I0464828

Egon Schiele: Paintings and Drawings

Paintings&Drawings, Volume 3

Jessica Findley

Published by Icon-m, 2014.

Egon Schiele: Paintings and Drawings
By Jessica Findley
Foreword by Jessica Findley
First Edition

Also by Jessica Findley

Paintings&Drawings
Egon Schiele: Paintings and Drawings

Standalone
Camille Corot: 130 Paintings
Antoine Watteau: 78 Paintings

Foreword

Egon Schiele (1890 - 1918) was an Austrian painter, a protégé of Gustav Klimt and important figurative painter of the early 20th century. The twisted body shapes and the expressive line that characterize his paintings and drawings mark the artist as one an earliest exponent of Expressionism. In Schiele's early years, he was strongly influenced by Klimt and Kokoschka but soon evolved into his own characteristic style. Some critics view Schiele's work as being grotesque, erotic, pornographic, or disturbing, focusing on sex, death, and discovery. Shiele answered to them in that way:

"To restrict the artist is a crime. It is to murder germinating life".

He was born in 1890 in Lower Austria as the third child in his family. His father was a rail-road civil servant who died in 1905. His uncle became his protector but did not support his artistic career. Nevertheless, Schiele entered the academy in Vienna where he quickly ran into difficulties with his teacher, the then famous Professor Griepenkerl.

In 1907 he met Gustav Klimt, whom he admired, who assisted him in obtaining his first commissions and who influenced his early drawing style. Following Klimt's suggestion, Schiele entered four paintings in the Vienna International Exhibition of 1909, where works by Oskar Kokoschka and Vincent Van Gogh were also shown. In the same year he left the academy and, with other young artists, formed the short-lived artist group "Neukunstgruppe"; however, the first exhibition was not successful. By 1910 he had found his own style with its strong emphasis on the contour line and vibrant colors.

In 1911 he moved to the small town of Krumau, where he painted a number of townscapes. His lifestyle caused problems in the town and he moved with his model Wally Neuziel to Neulengbach where in 1912 he was arrested and charged with immorality and seduction. Some of his drawings were confiscated; one was even burned by the judge in the courtroom. He spent 24 traumatic days in jail and returned to Vienna upon his release.

His first important exhibitions were held in Germany: in 1913 in the famous Galerie Goltz in Munich and in the Folkwangmuseum in Hagen, followed by one-man exhibits in Hamburg, Breslau, Stuttgart, and Berlin, where the Expressionist journal Die Aktion published his drawings as well as his poetry. In 1915 he married Edith Harms, and a few days later he was drafted into the army. After having been assigned to guard Russian prisoners of war, the Die Aktion journal published a special issue with his drawings and the Berlin Sezession exhibited his works.

In 1917 he was transferred to the Army Museum in Vienna, which provided him with some time to paint again. A portfolio of 12 drawing reproductions was published. He was invited to participate in exhibits in Munich, Dresden, Amsterdam, and Stockholm, but his poverty remained unchanged. The first truly great success came in 1918 with his exhibit at the Vienna Secession (no less than 19 paintings and several drawings). He received a number of commissions, and 25 of his works were exhibited in Zurich. Shortly thereafter, however, his wife—who was expecting a child-died of the Spanish influenza epidemic, and three days later the artist succumbed to the same disease.

Schiele's dominating theme was the human body, which he depicts in truly singular forms. Likewise in his paintings of children he emphasized their awkward bodies and their earnest eyes, and yet, the impact of these works on the viewer is very strong because the depictions are forthright and direct. Even his marvelous townscapes frequently lack perspective dimensions and let the windows of the houses appear like blind eyes; they are expressions of the artist's mood more than topographical depictions; they are images of fall—with isolated, dry trees standing in the cold wind.

Schiele's symbolic works, such as "Death and the Maiden," "The Hermits," or even such seemingly happy themes as "Mother with Two Children," show the same penetrating insight for which his portraits have become famous. His many self-portraits are proof of his continuous struggle with what he considered the soul of the arts: the depiction of that truth which lies below the surface. While the subject matter seems to be depressing, his works prove otherwise. The extraordinary ability to form the three dimensional body through dominating contour lines, his choice of very strong and forthright colors, the frequently ambiguous spaces, and his extraordinary sensitivity, which transforms even a seemingly quick drawing into a complete work of art, have allowed Schiele's fame to continue to grow.

He focused on portraits of others as well as himself. In his later years, while he still worked often with nudes, they were done in a more realist fashion. Schiele made many drawings, some of which were extremely erotic. During his short but highly prolific career which ended with his premature death, Schiele created more than three thousand works on paper and approximately three hundred paintings.

With his signature graphic style, embrace of figural distortion, and bold defiance of conventional norms of beauty, Egon Schiele was one of the leading figures of Austrian Expressionism.

Paintings

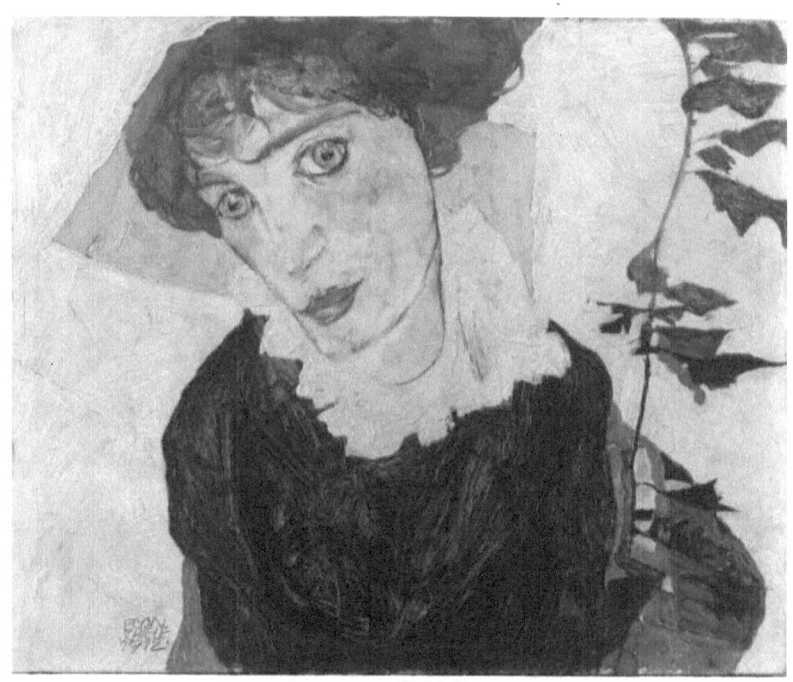

Portrait of Wally
1912, Oil on panel, 32.7 x 39.8 cm, Leopold Museum, Vienna
Portrait of Wally is an oil painting by Austrian painter Egon Schiele of Valerie "Wally" Neuzil, a woman he met in 1911 when she was 17 years old and who was a model for a number of Schiele's most striking paintings. The painting was purchased by Rudolf Leopold in 1954 and became part of the collection of the Leopold Museum when it was established by the Austrian government, purchasing 5,000 pieces that Leopold had owned.

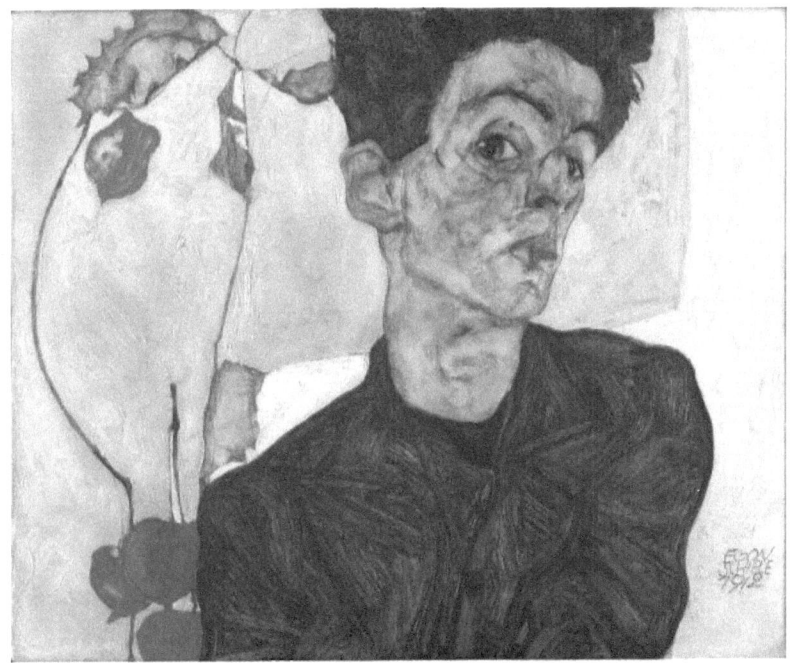

Self-Portrait with Chinese lantern plant
1912, Oil on canvas, Leopold Museum, Vienna
This is perhaps Schiele's most celebrated self-portrait, and certainly the most storied. In this work, painted during a time in which he was participating in numerous exhibitions, Schiele gazes directly at the viewer, his expression suggesting a confidence in his artistic gifts. Although Schiele deploys less distortion than in other self-portraits, the painting refuses to idealize its subject, featuring scars and other lines characteristic of the contoured manner of the artist's drawing style.

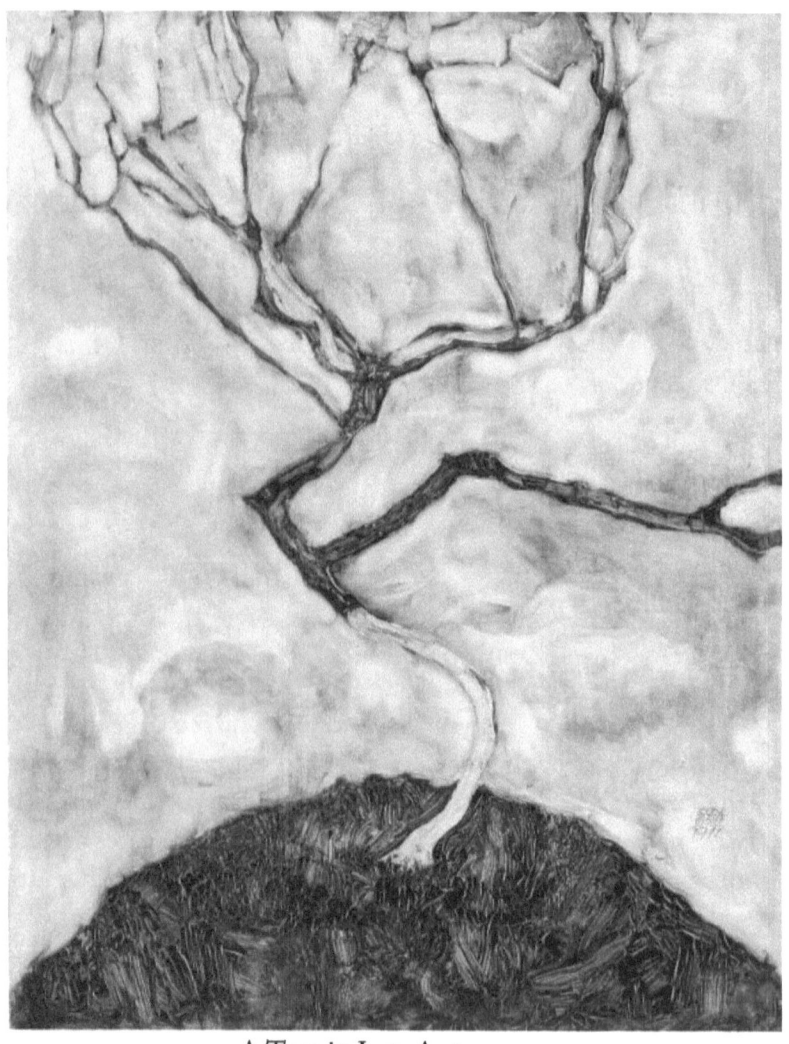

A Tree in Late Autumn
1911, Oil on wood, 42 x 33.35 cm, Leopold Museum (Austria)

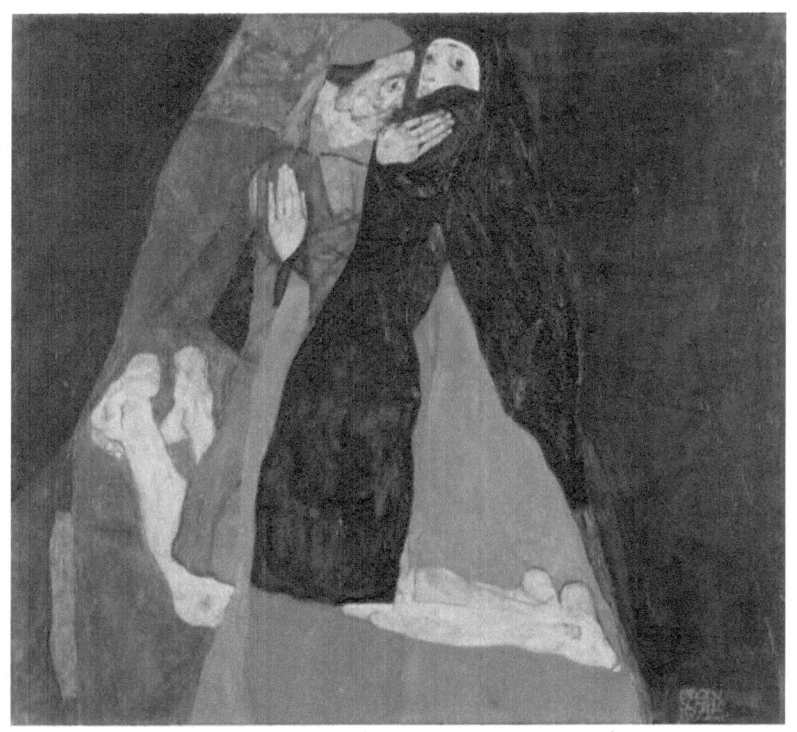

Cardinal and Nun (also known as Caress)
1912, Oil on canvas, Leopold Museum, Vienna

Schiele's painting Cardinal and Nun of 1912 is a paraphrase of Gustav Klimt'sKiss, which had been created five years prior. Everything about Klimt's painting that was positive, however, is transformed here into its darker manifestation: the gold background is turned black, the gentle embrace has given way the violent clutching of the two delicate, praying hands, and the sensual expression on the face of Klimt's woman has become a nun's distraught glance. Schiele called the painting of this strange embrace Liebkosung, or "The Caress".

The contrast between the Cardinal's bare, muscular legs and the nun's ecclesiastic garb, between her sober black and his luminous red, reveals the power of sexual desire—which seems quite alienating indeed in the painting's Catholic context. Her posture and facial expression indicate fear—and it remains uncertain whether it is fear of being discovered, of the cardinal, or of sexuality in general. Upon Schiele's marriage in 1915, in any case, his portraits of women changed: they became calmer, and their inherent sexuality lost both its terrifying quality and its unsettling force.

EGON SCHIELE

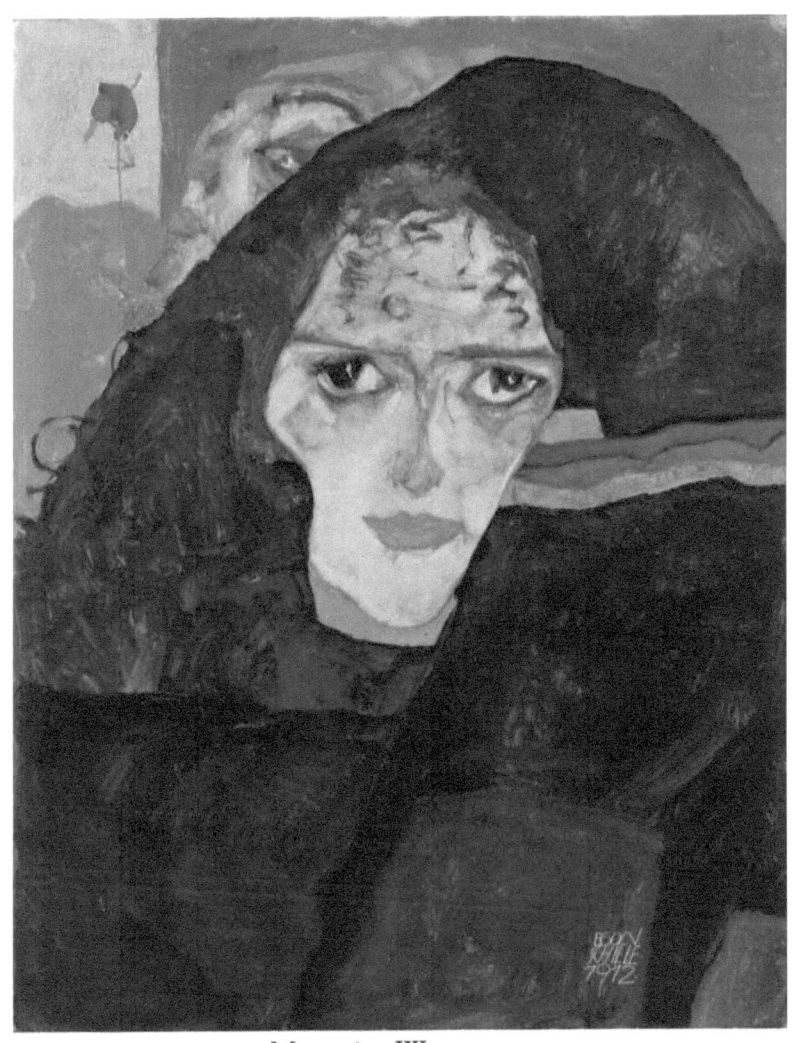

Mourning Woman
1912, Oil on canvas

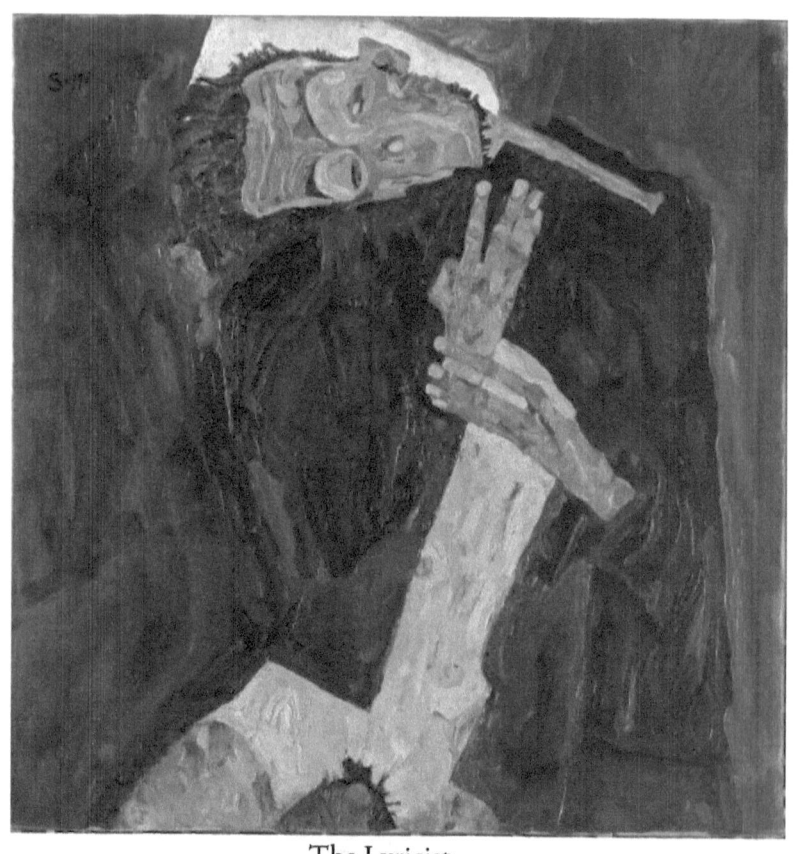

The Lyricist
1911, Oil on canvas

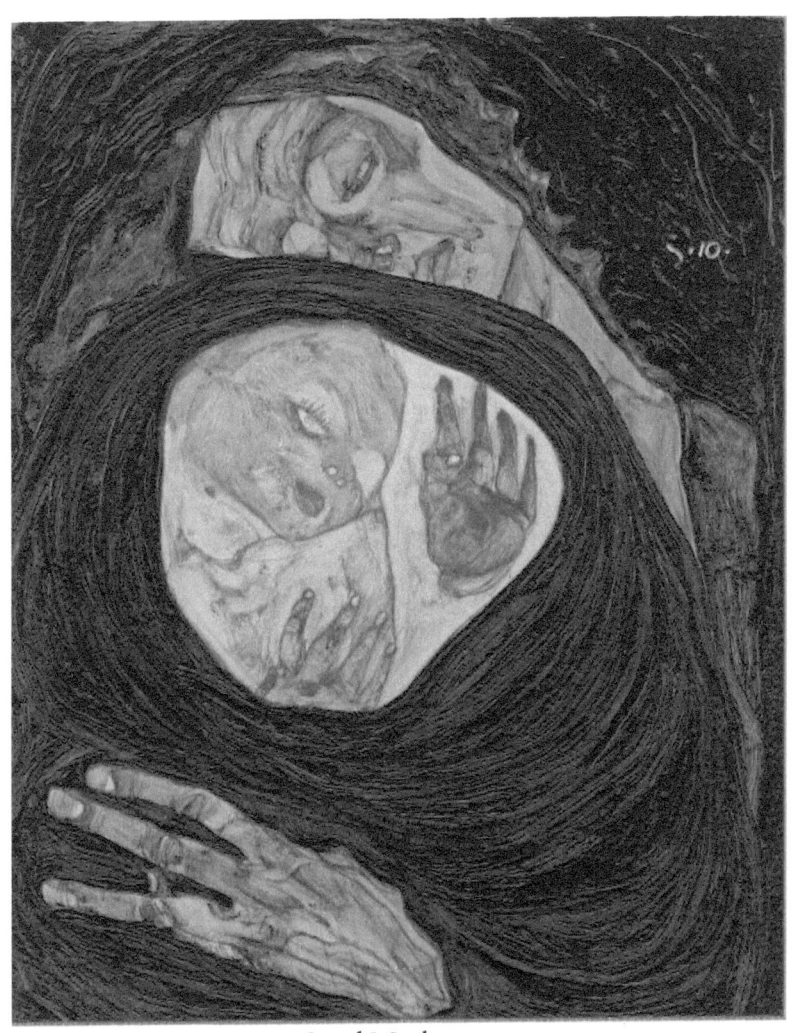

Dead Mother
1910, Oil on board, Private collection

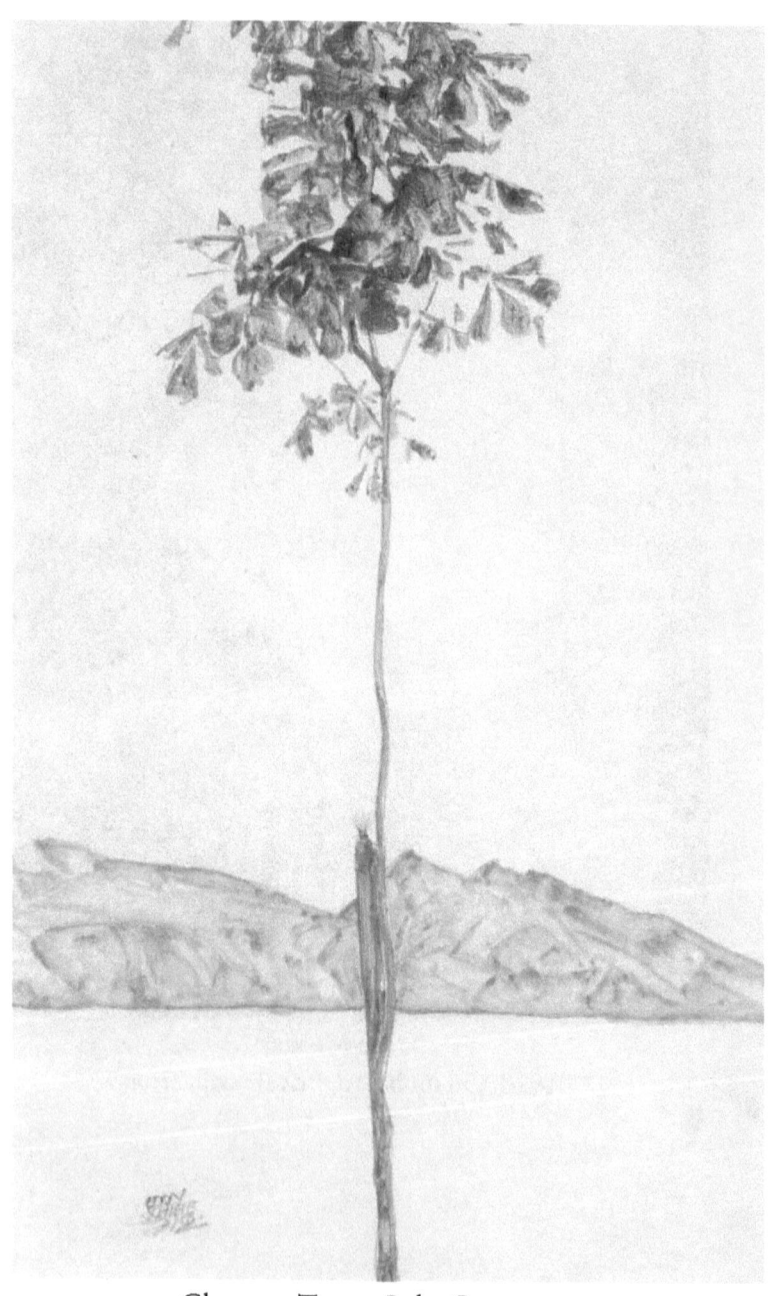

Jessica Findley

Chestnut Tree at Lake Constance
1911, Oil on canvas

EGON SCHIELE

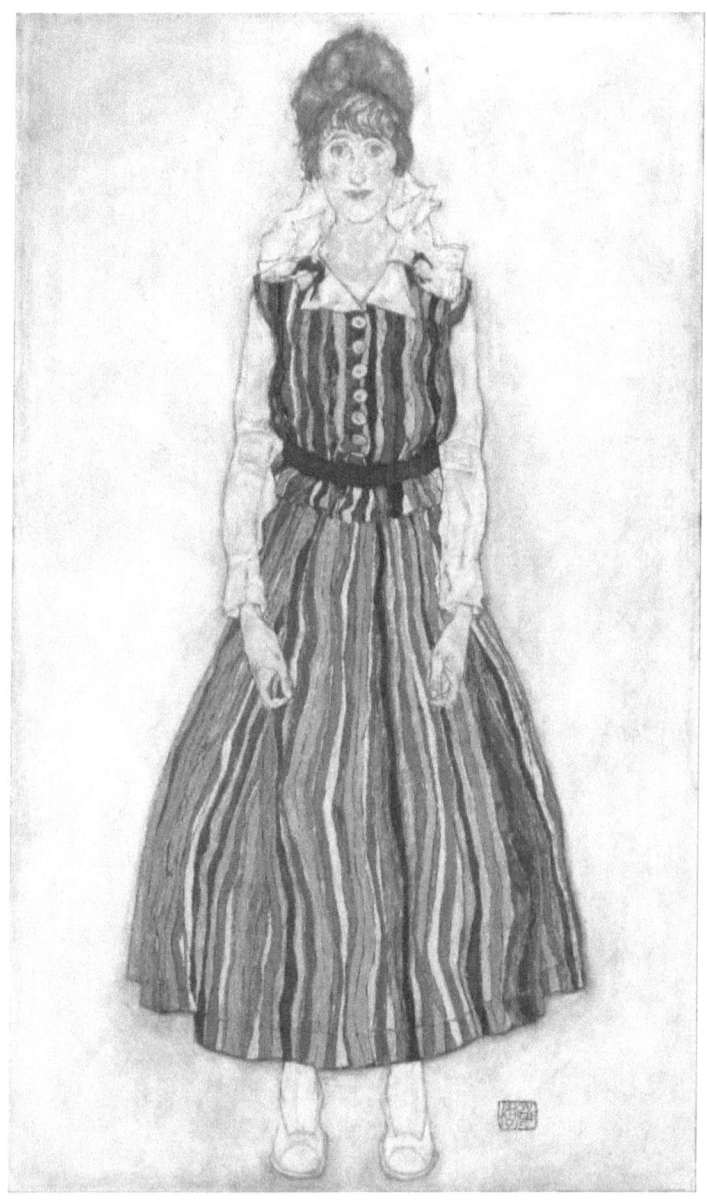

Portrait of Edith Schiele in a Striped Dress
1915, Oil on canvas, Haags Gemeentemuseum (Netherlands)

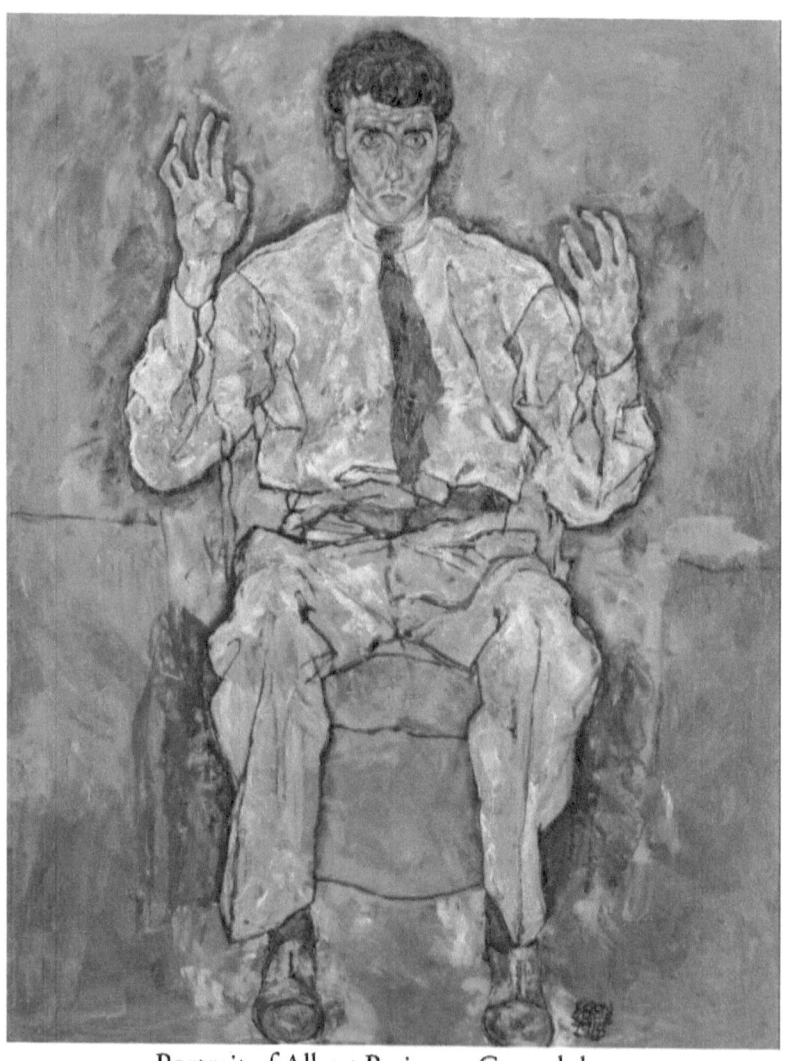

Jessica Findley

Portrait of Albert Paris von Gutersloh
1918, Oil on canvas, 109.5 x139.5 cm, Minneapolis Institute of
Arts (United States)
Detail

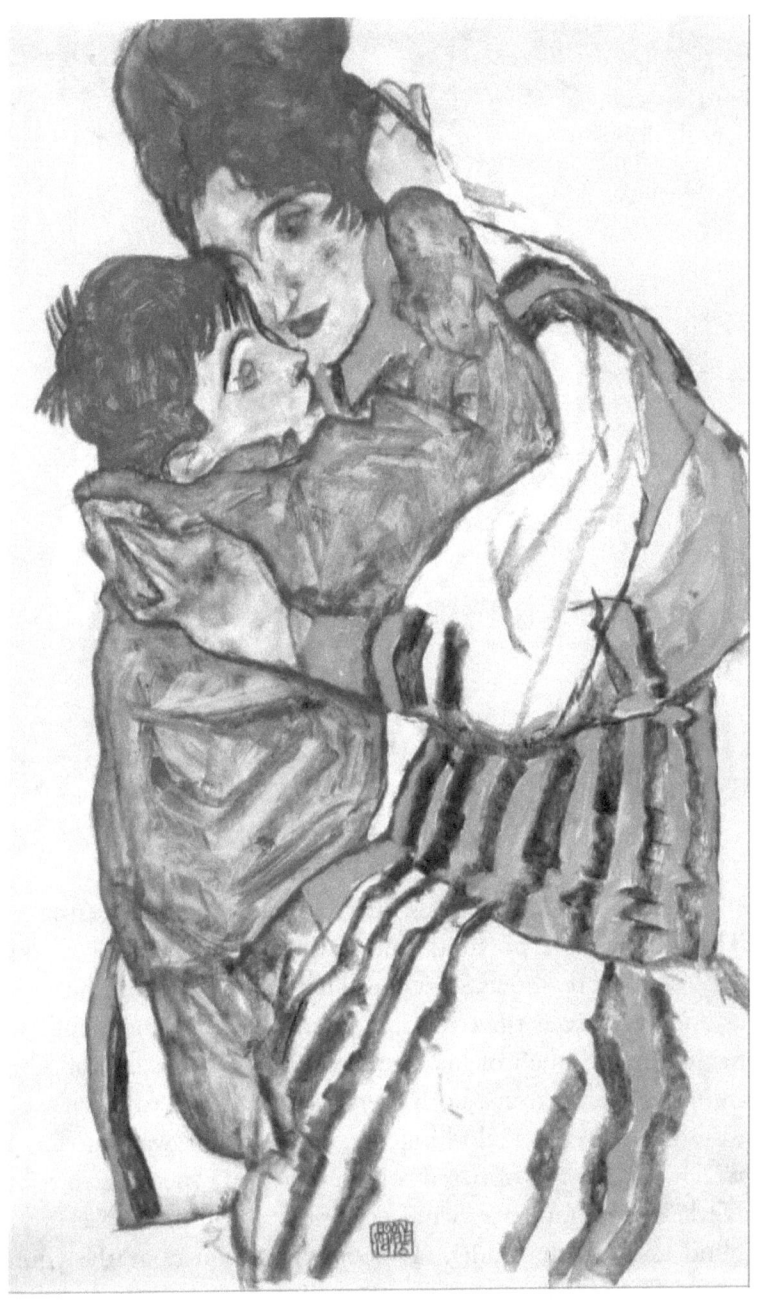

Schiele's Wife with Her Little Nephew
1915, Watercolor

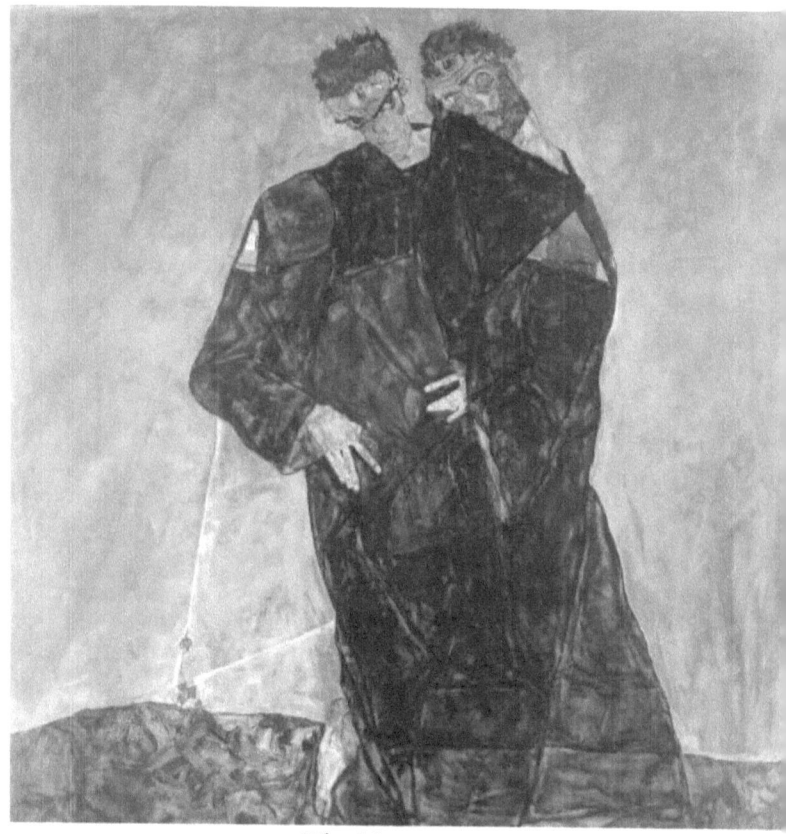

The Hermits
1912, Oil on canvas, The Leopold Museum, Vienna

This rare double portrait, among the most allegorical works in Schiele's oeuvre, shows Schiele and Klimt standing together, nearly as one. As close as the two men were, and for all their similarities, Schiele spent much of his career seeking to break free of Klimt's influence. In Hermits, both men wear their signature long black caftans, an item of clothing for which Klimt was known, and which Schiele appropriated for his own work, perhaps in tribute. Never one for modesty, Schiele positions Klimt in the background, blind and mostly hidden, as if being consumed by the younger artist. The resulting form evokes the image of a single dark figure, indicating the confident successor Schiele assuming the mantel of the old master. The hermit motif also evokes Schiele's existential conception of the artist as a figure existing at the margins of society.

Jessica Findley

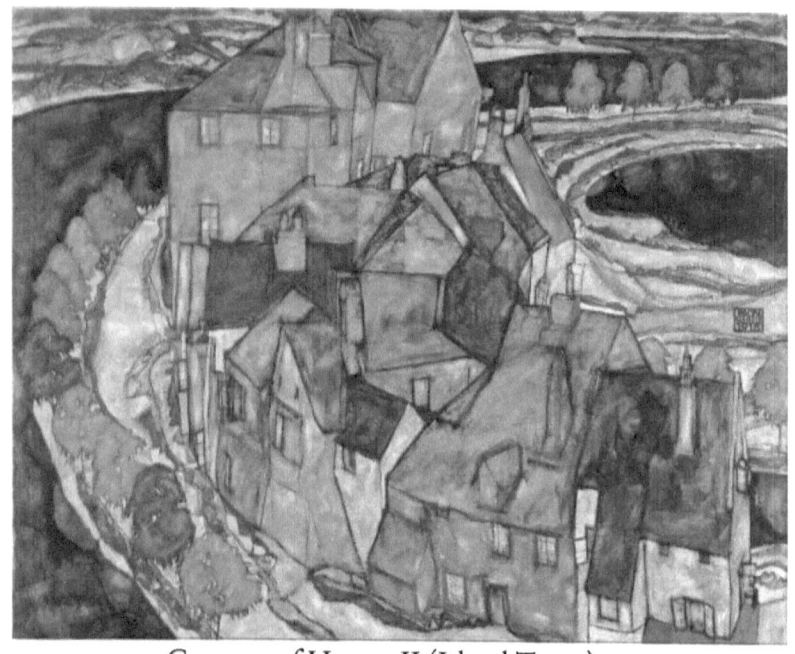

Crescent of Houses II (Island Town)
1915, Oil on canvas

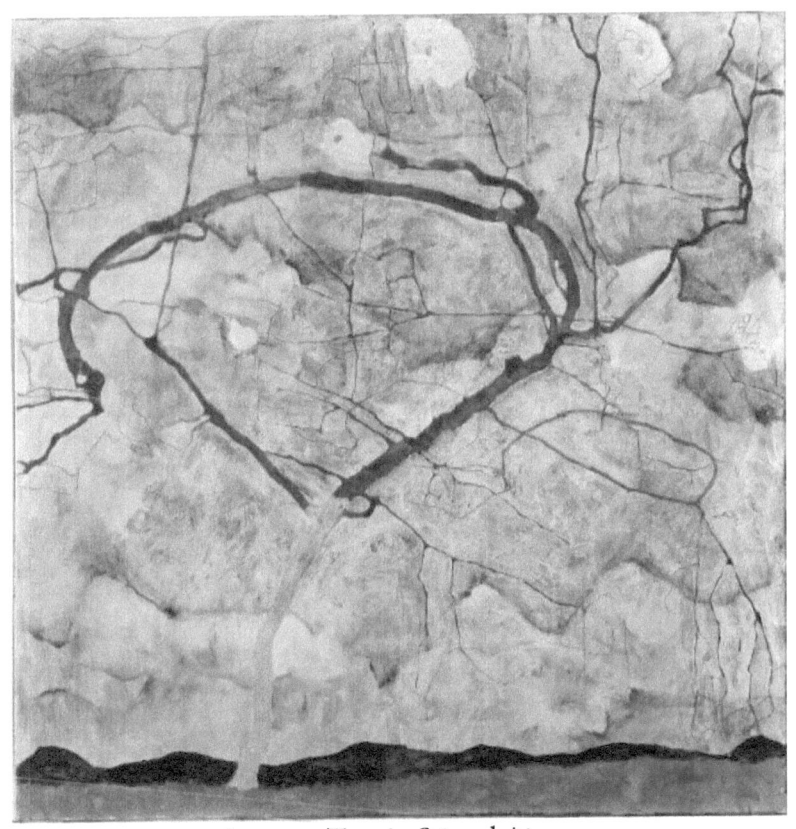

Autumn Tree in Stirred Air
1912, Oil on canvas

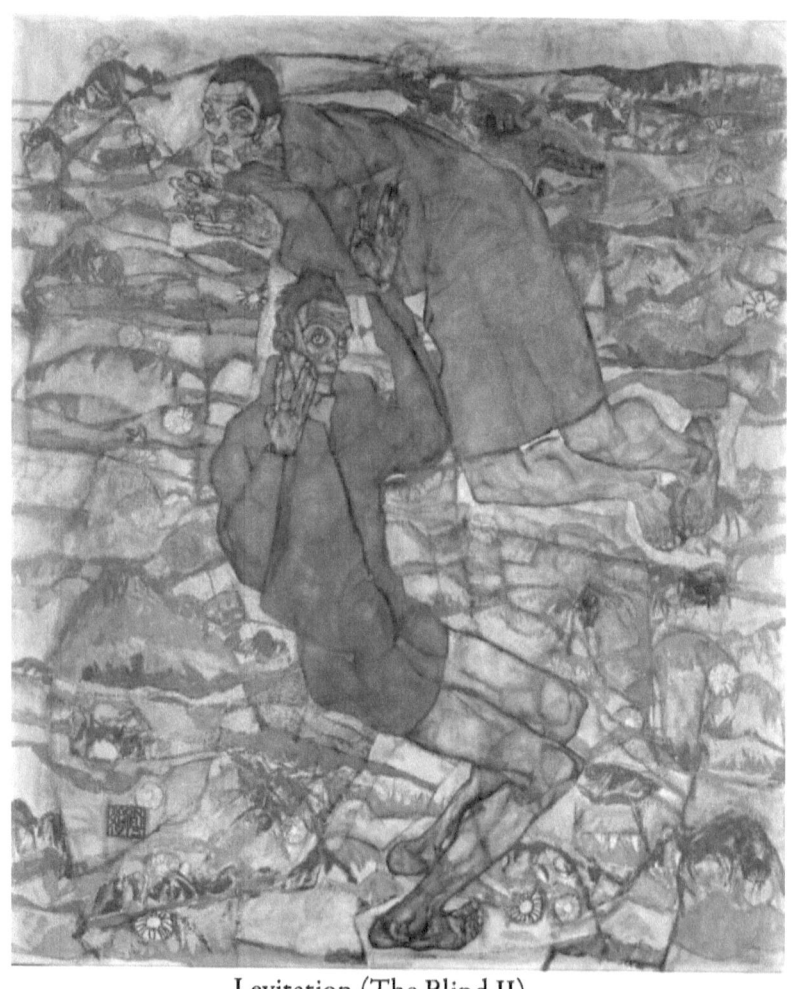

Levitation (The Blind II)
1915, Oil on canvas

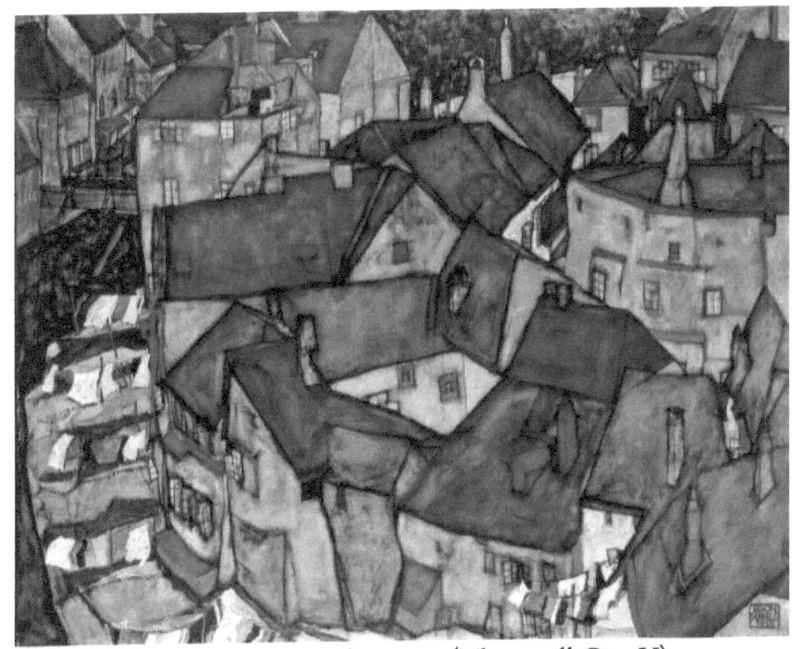

Krumau - Crescent of Houses (The small City V)
1915, Oil on canvas

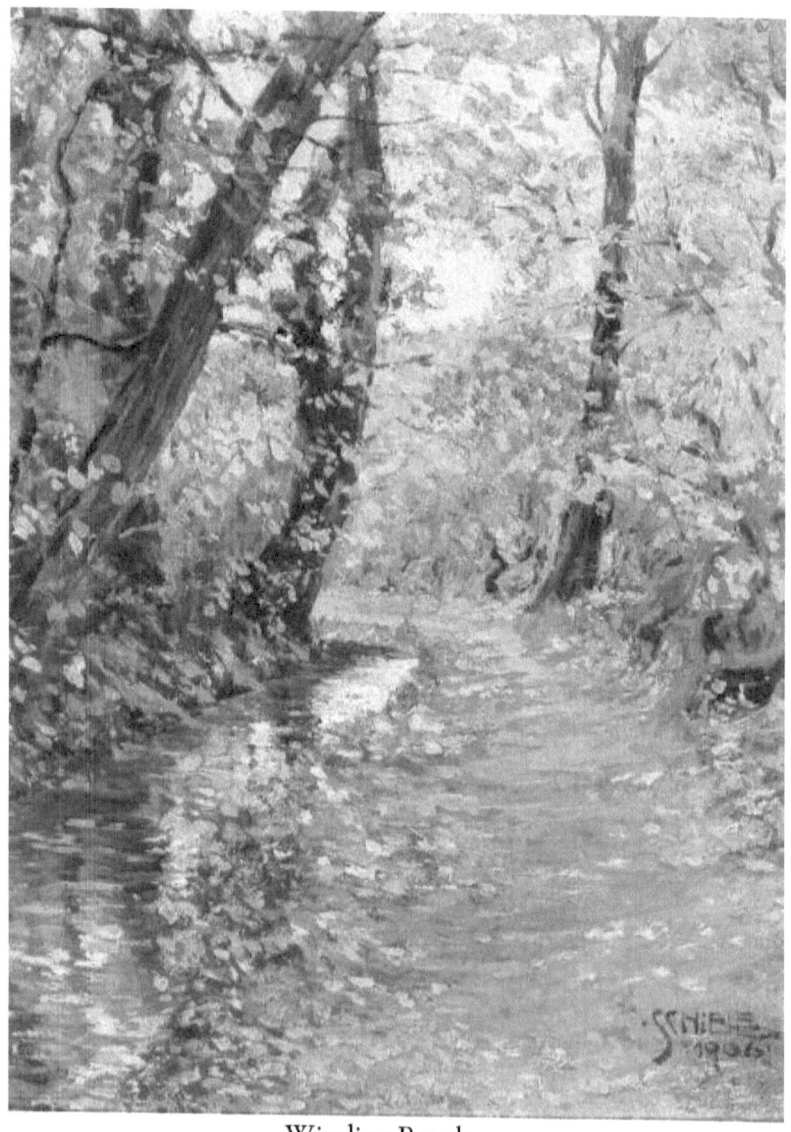

Winding Brook
1906, Oil on panel, 30.48 x 24.13 cm, Private collection

EGON SCHIELE

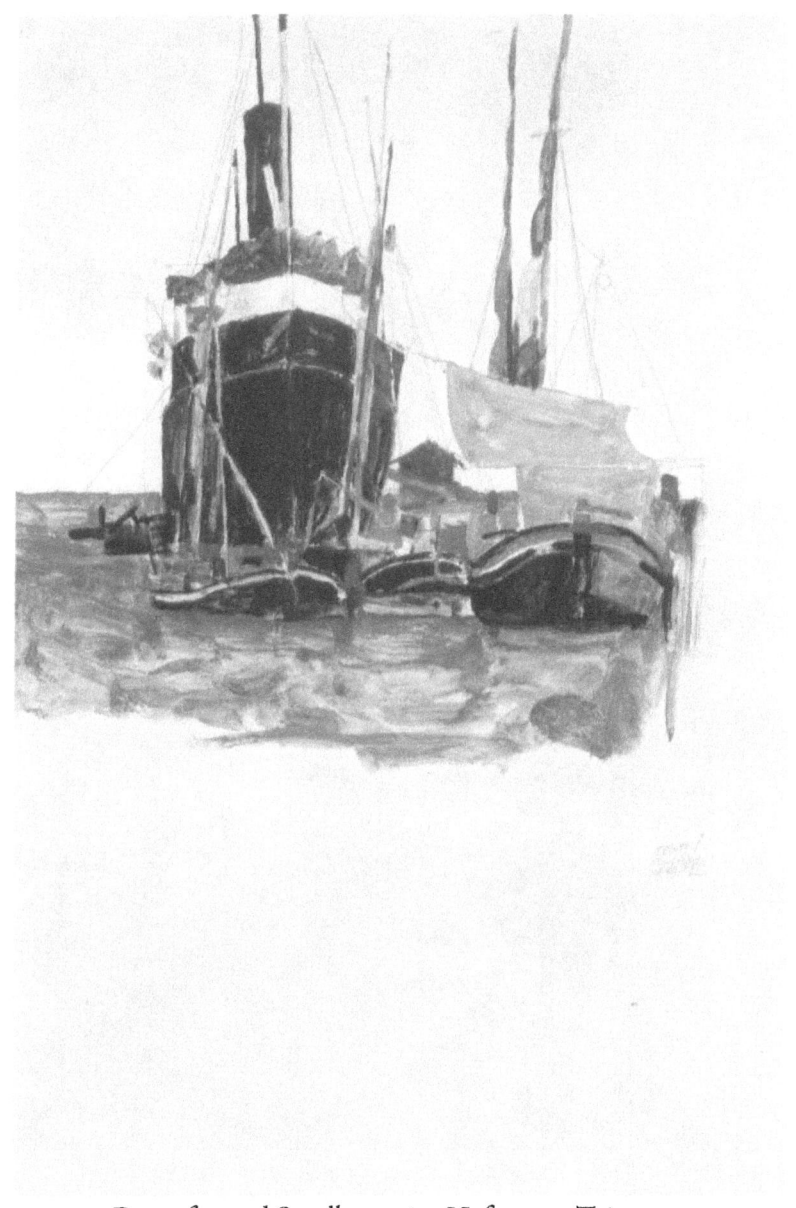

Dampfer und Segelboote im Hafen von Triest
1912, watercolor, pencil and gouache on japan paper, grundiert

Jessica Findley

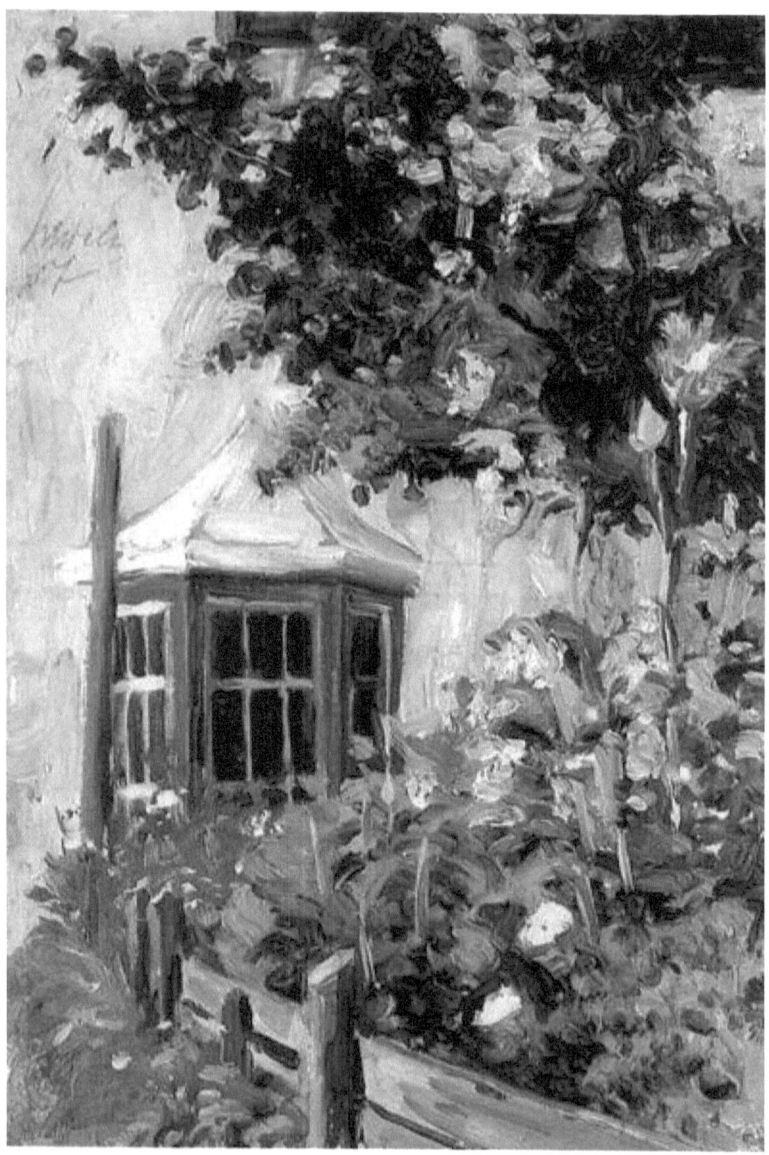

House with a Bay Window in the Garden
1907, Oil on canvas, 36 x 26.5 cm, Private collection

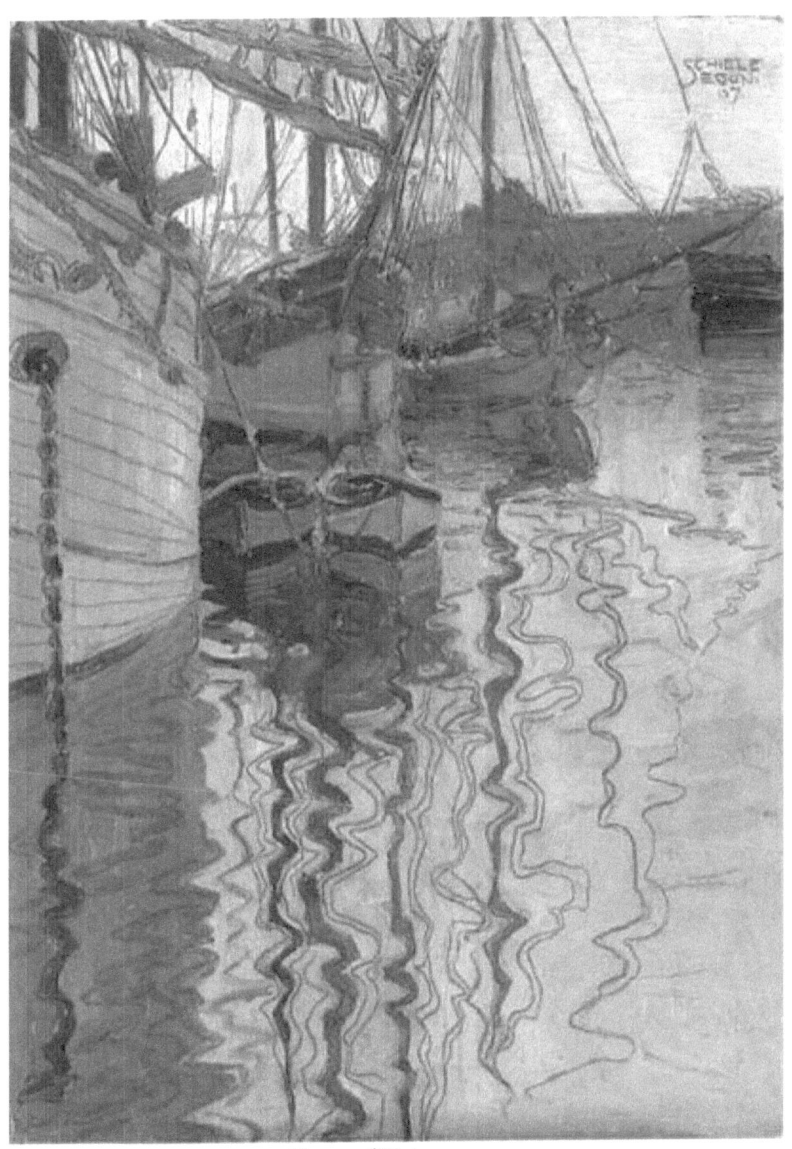

Port of Trieste
1907, Oil and pencil on cardboard, 24.6 x 18 cm, Private
collection

1907 was an innovative year for the seventeen year old Schiele. While still a student at the Vienna Academy he had already outgrown the place, its doctrines and its teachers and was increasingly leaning towards the more radical and experimental art of the Viennese Secession - in particular that of its leader Gustav Klimt. It was in 1907 that Schiele first got to know Klimt - the artist 'through' whom, as he later said, he was to reach his own unique style.

Hafen von Triest is one of Schiele's finest oil paintings from this important year. It is also perhaps the very first of his works to suggest the future direction that his art would take. In Hafen von Triest Schiele not only demonstrates his accomplished mastery of formal technique but in the Expressionistic styling of lines reflected in the water - made using the unorthodox technique of scoring the wet paint with a pencil or the wrong end of the brush - something daring and experimental. For the first time in an oil painting Schiele's precocious genius as a draughtsman is clearly in evidence in the assured ease with which these distinct and soon to be familiar fluid angular lines masterfully describe the watery reflection of the masts and rigging.

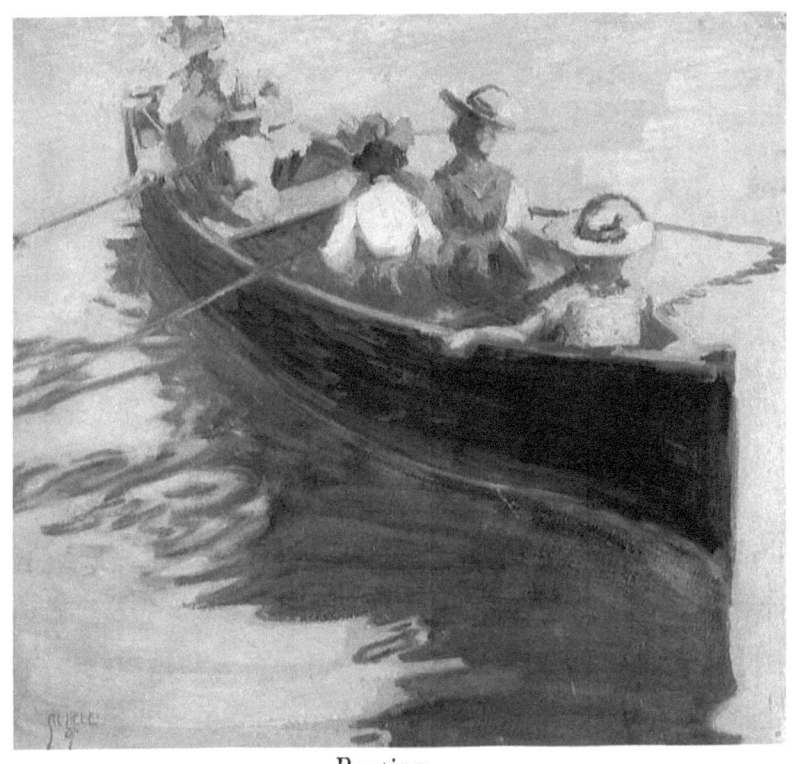

Boating
1907, Oil on cardboard, Private collection

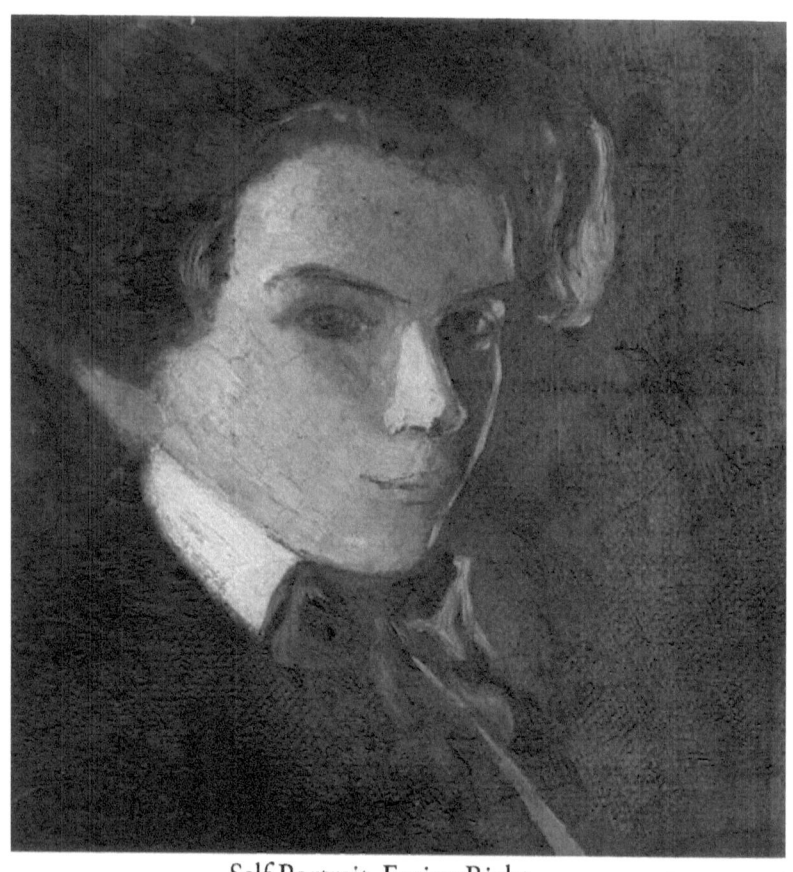

Self Portrait, Facing Right
1907, Oil on card, 32.4 x 31.2 cm, Private collection

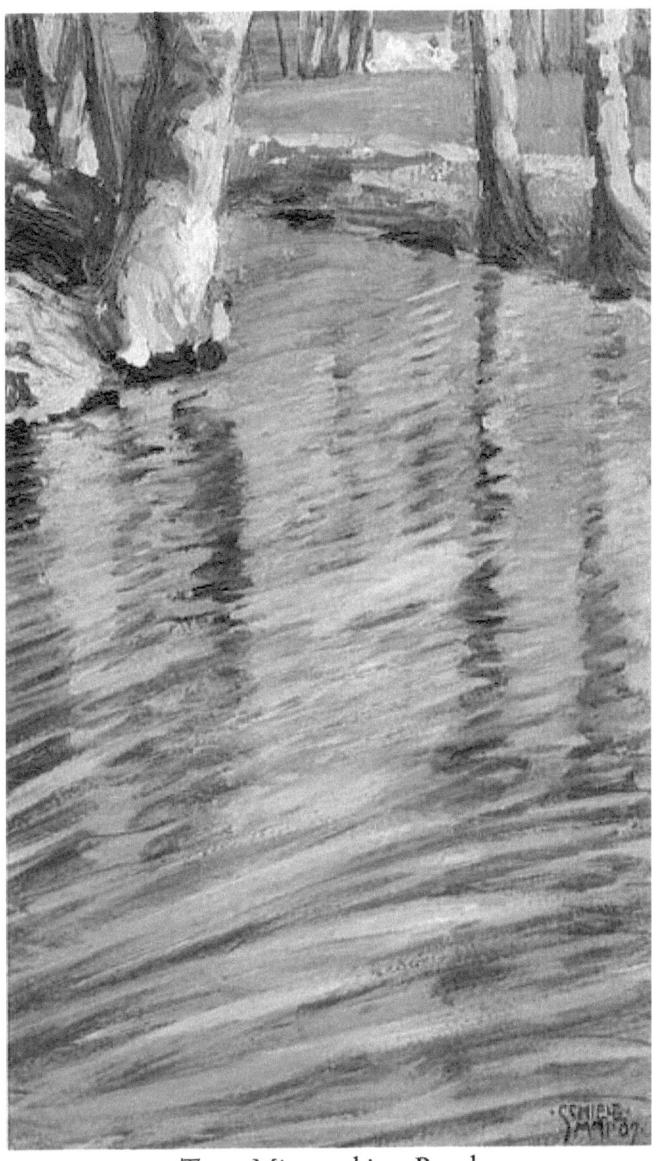

Trees Mirrored in a Pond
1907, Oil on cardboard, private collection

Jessica Findley

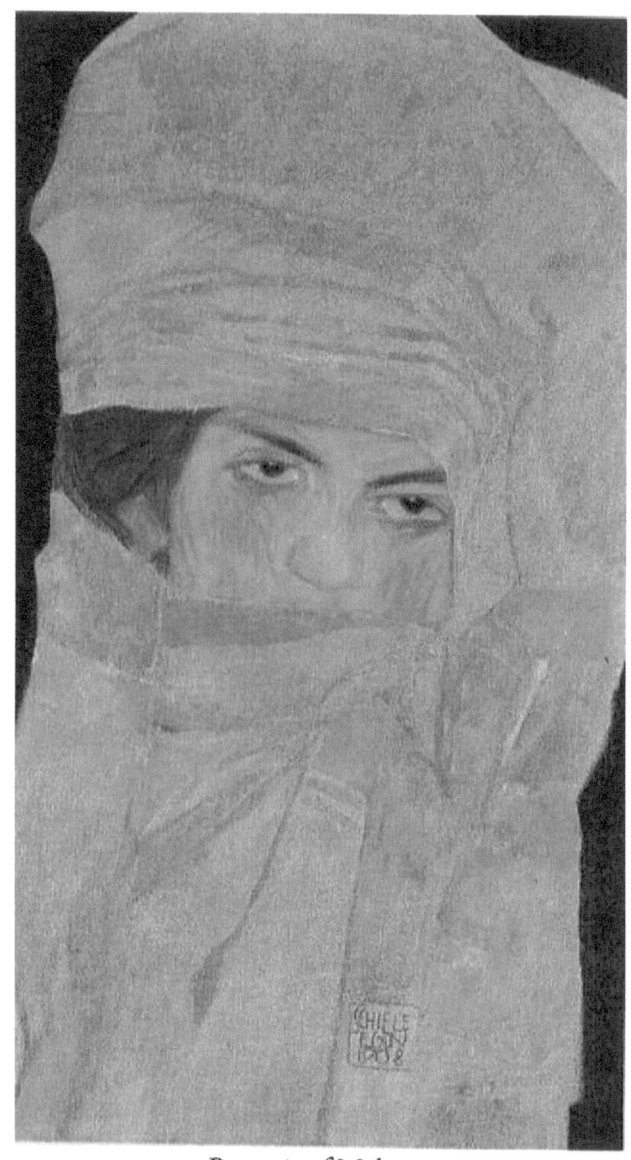

Portrait of Melanie
1908, Oil on canvas, Private collection

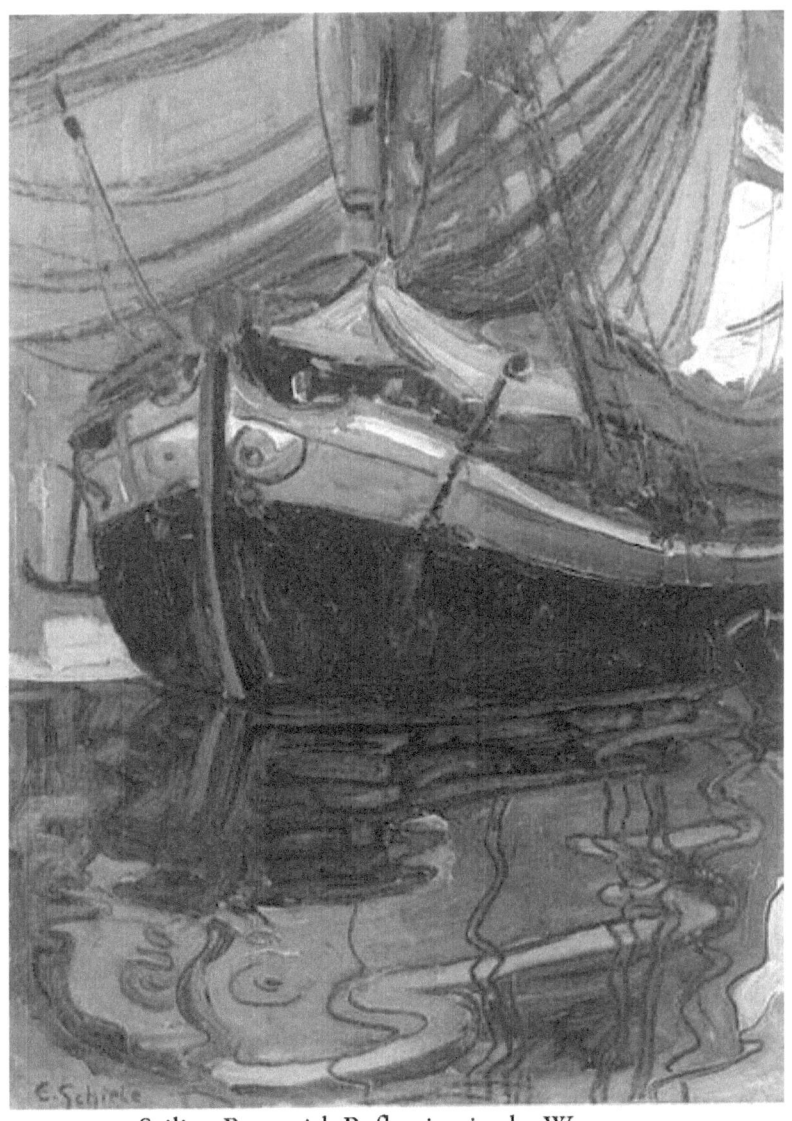

Sailing Boat with Reflection in the Water
1908, Oil and pencil on board, 24.1 x 17.8 cm, private
collection

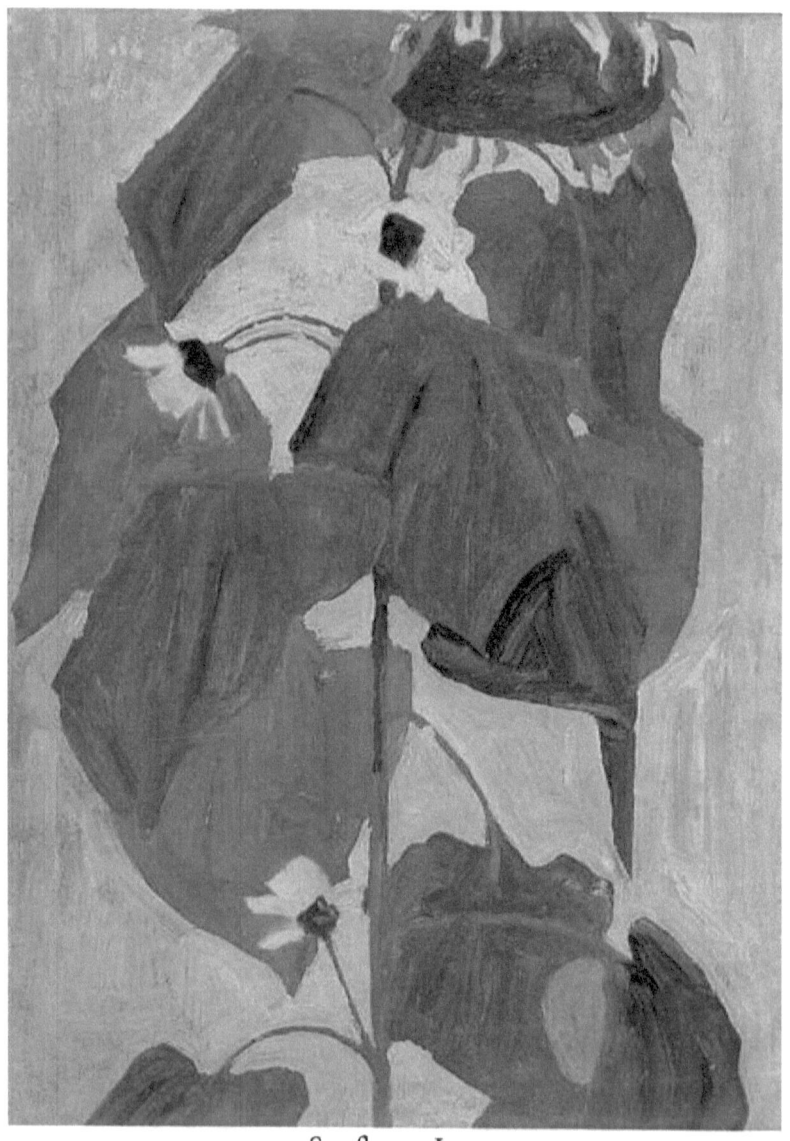

Sunflower I
1908, Oil on cardboard, Niedersaechsisches Landesmuseum
(Germany)

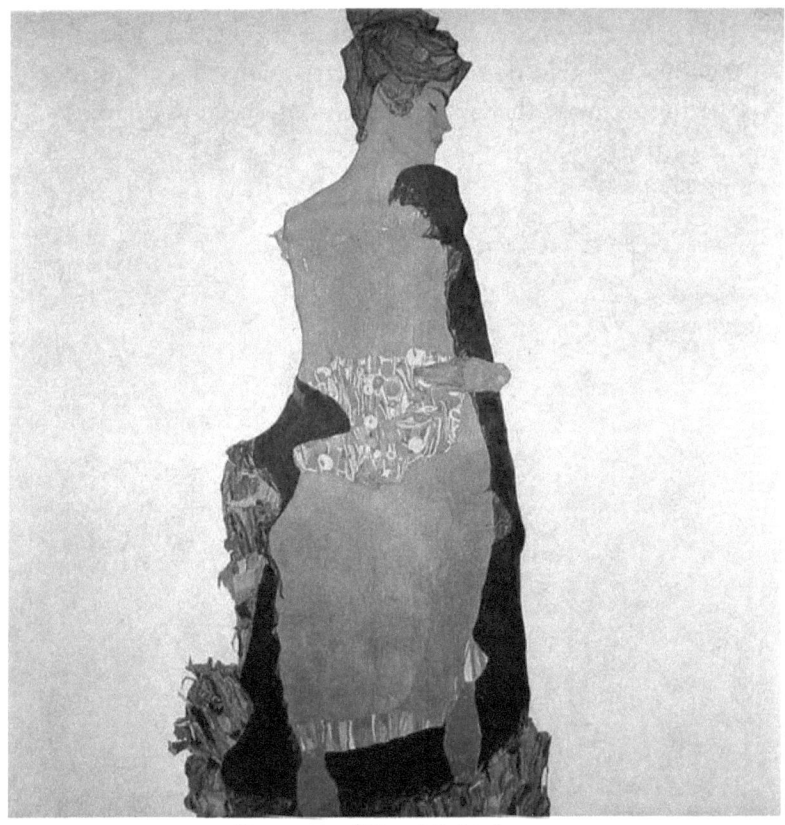

Portrait of Gerti Schiele
1909, Oil, silver, gold-bronze paint, and pencil on canvas, The
Museum of Modern Art, New York

This is one of Schiele's many portraits of his younger sister, Gerti,
the artist's favorite model during his early career and the member
of his family with whom he was the closest. Painted when Gerti
was a teenager, this early portrait demonstrates both the strong
stylistic link between Schiele's work and that of Klimt, as well as
the shift away from the style of his mentor. In her pose and
adornment composed from a series of flat patches with gold and
silver accents, Gerti's figure is reminiscent of Klimt's works such as
Portrait of Adele Bloch-Bauer (1907). But the image is not so
much decorative as static and soft, as if Schiele were casting his

sitter in clay. In addition, Schiele replaced Klimt's richly shimmering, gold-dominated palette with more muted colors, creating an image that appears dried-out, suggestive of decay rather than growth.

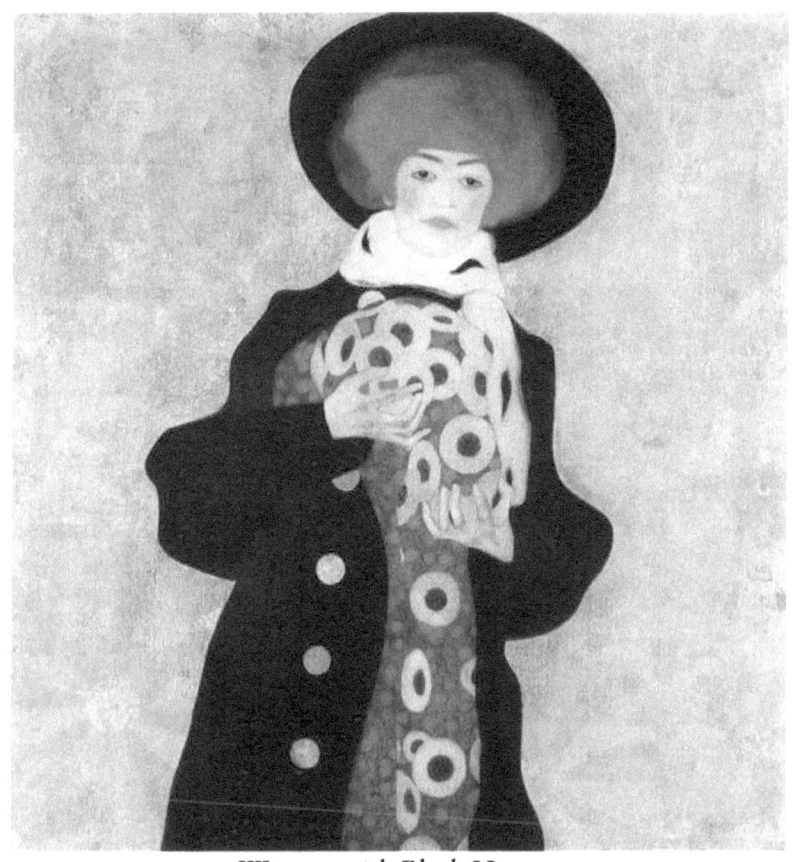

Woman with Black Hat
1909, Oil and metallic paint on canvas, 100 x 99.7 cm, Private
collection

Jessica Findley

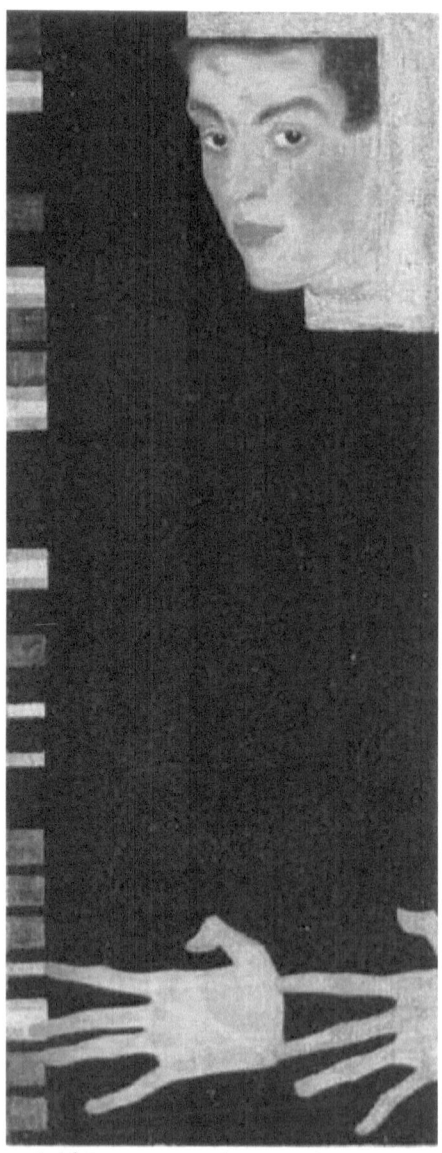

Self-Portrait with Spread Fingers
1909, Oil on metallic paint on canvas, 71.5 x 27.5 cm, Private
collection

1909 was the year of Egon Schiele's great breakthrough to artistic maturity. Although only nineteen years old and, until the summer of the year, still a student at the Viennese Academy of Art, Schiele's prodigious talent had already asserted itself to the point where he had become recognized by Gustav Klimt and many others as one of the greatest hopes for the future of Austrian art. Selbstbildnis mit gespreizten Fingern (Self-Portrait with Spread Fingers) is an important early work from late 1909 that reveals Schiele already beginning to move beyond the dominant influence of his mentor Klimt towards a new, more existentially aware Expressionist art.

Still reliant on Klimt's style in many ways, this painting takes the thin elongated format and decorative style of several of Klimt's recent works, most notably Judith II, also of 1909. Like this painting, but going even further in a way that anticipates much of his later work, the artist has chosen to render his self-image solely through a representation of his face and his expressively gesticulating hands. Unlike Klimt, who has concentrated on these features in Judith II, but incorporated them into sumptuous decorative motif of high Secessionist style, Schiele has completely isolated these two features by contrasting them against a black void-like background.

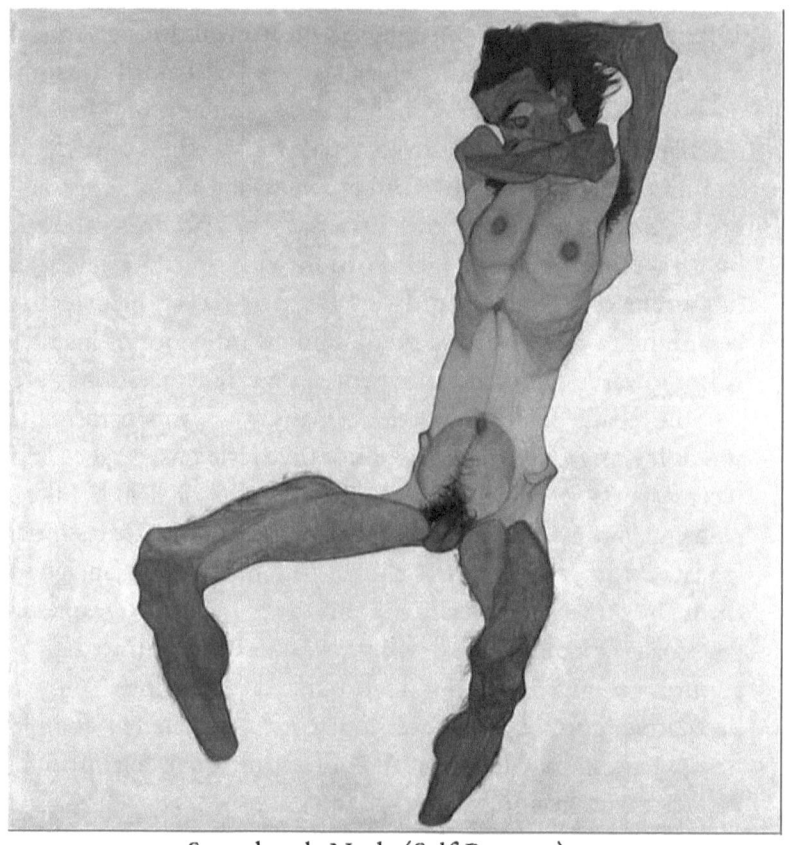

Seated male Nude (Self-Portrait)
1910, Oil on canvas, 152.5 x 150 cm, Leopold Museum,
Vienna, Austria

Here, the only 20-year-old Egon Schiele shows himself to be an artist whose development is already impressively complete, having created in this self-nude a composition which is most disturbing but at the same time well-considered and well-balanced; in terms of its dramatic expressivity, this work was hardly to be exceeded later on.

The depicted yellow-green body contorts unnaturally and thus seems somehow locked inside itself. Indeed, the figure seems to have no way of making contact with its environment, since—in this painting—there quite simply is none: it was with quite some courage that the young Schiele placed himself on this empty, white canvas. Prior to this work, such a radical reduction of the background had hardly ever been done.

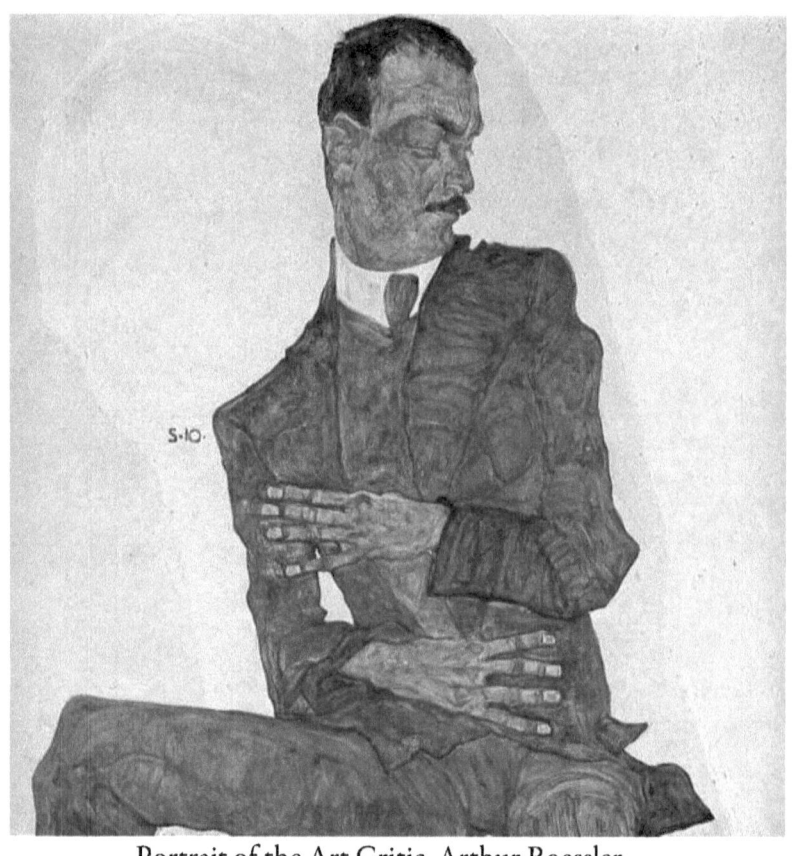

Portrait of the Art Critic, Arthur Roessler
1910, Oil on canvas, Kunsthistorisches Museum, Vienna
(Austria)

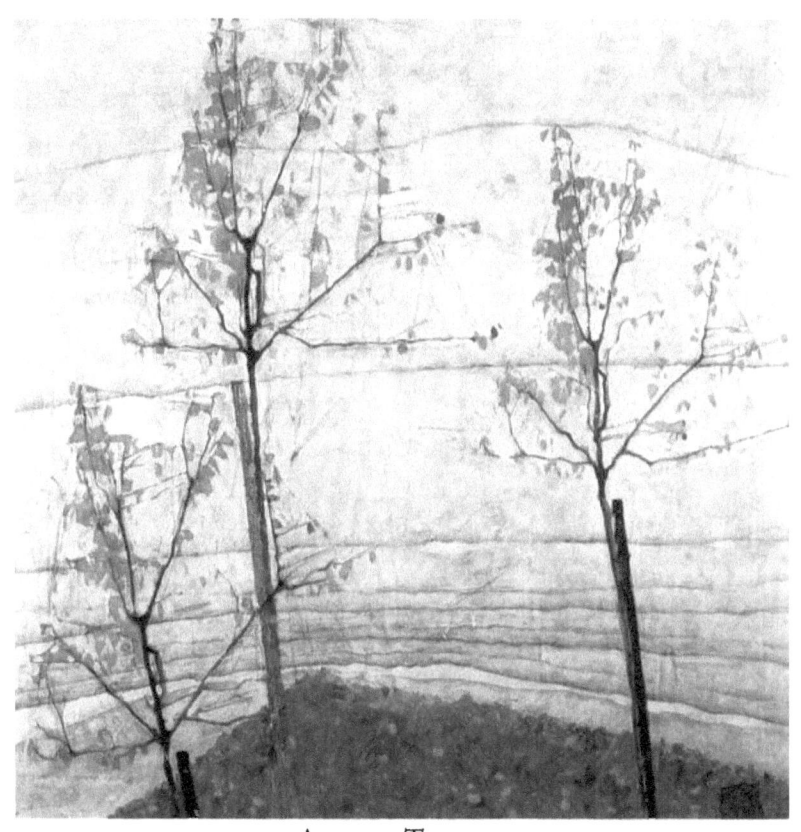

Autumn Trees
1911, Oil on canvas, 79.5 x 80 cm, Private collection

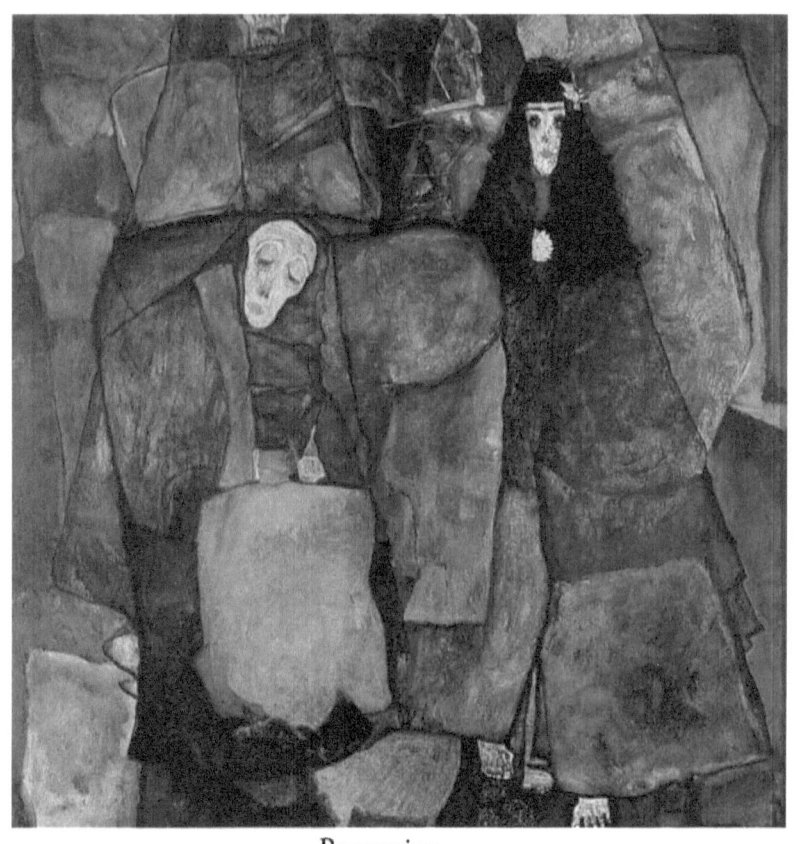

Procession
1911, Oil on canvas, 100 x 100 cm, Private collection

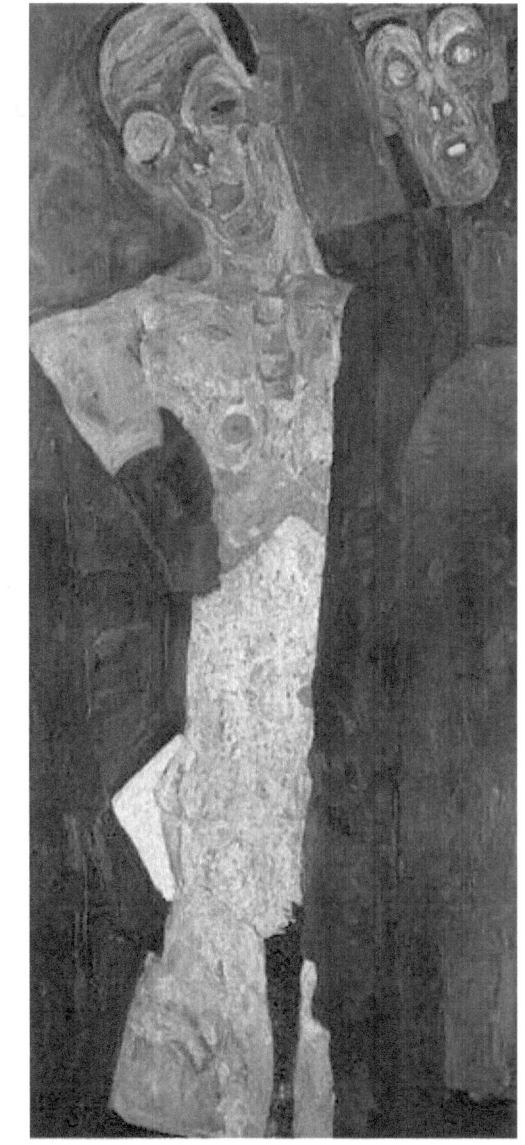

Prophets (also known as Double Self Portrait)
1911, Oil on canvas, Staatsgalerie Stuttgart (Germany)

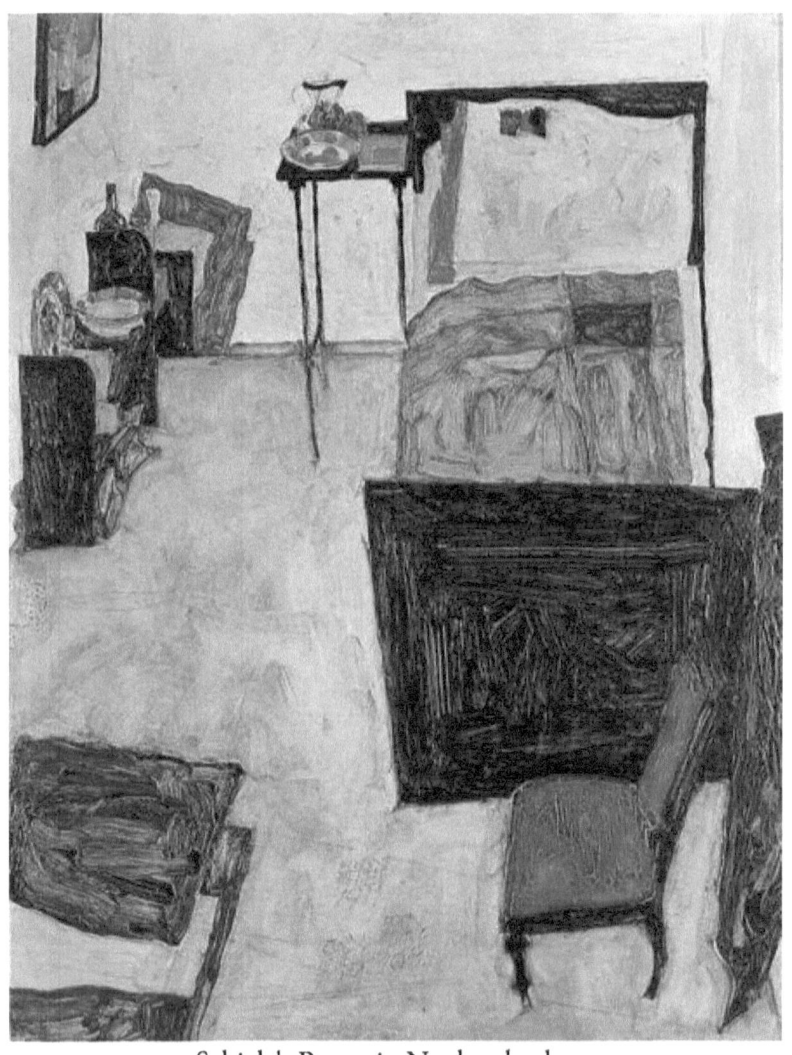

Schiele's Room in Neulengbach
1911, Oil on panel, Kunsthistorisches Museum, Vienna
(Austria)

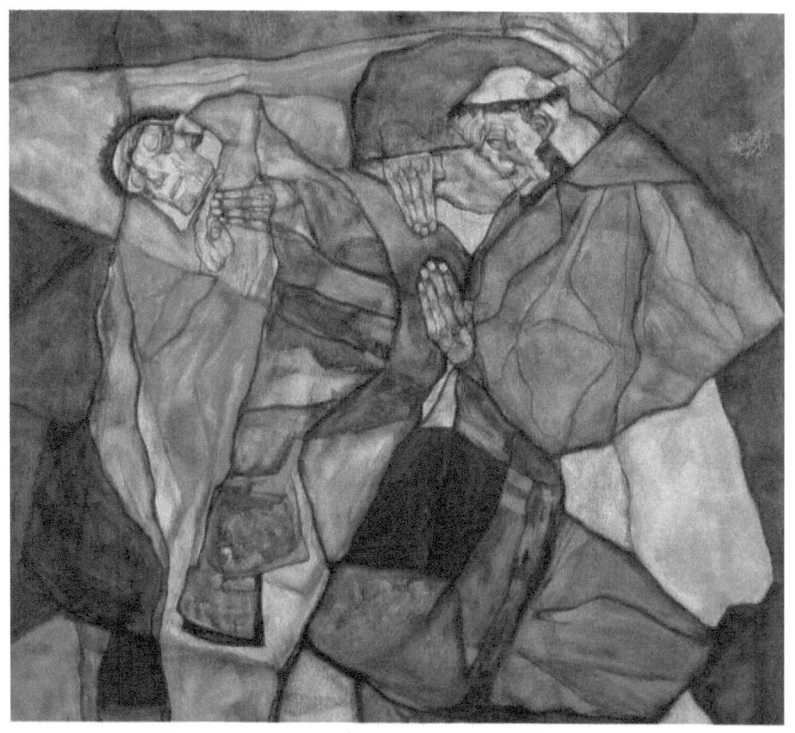

Agony
1912, Oil on canvas, 70 x 80 cm, Neue Pinakothek - Munich

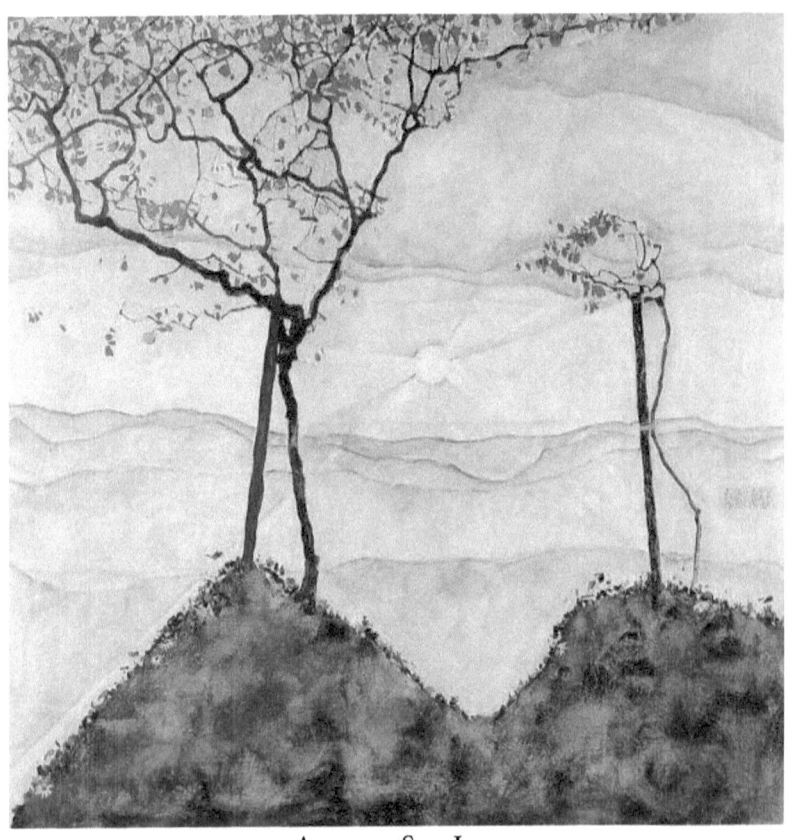

Autumn Sun I
1912, Oil on canvas, 80.2 x 80.5 cm, Private collection

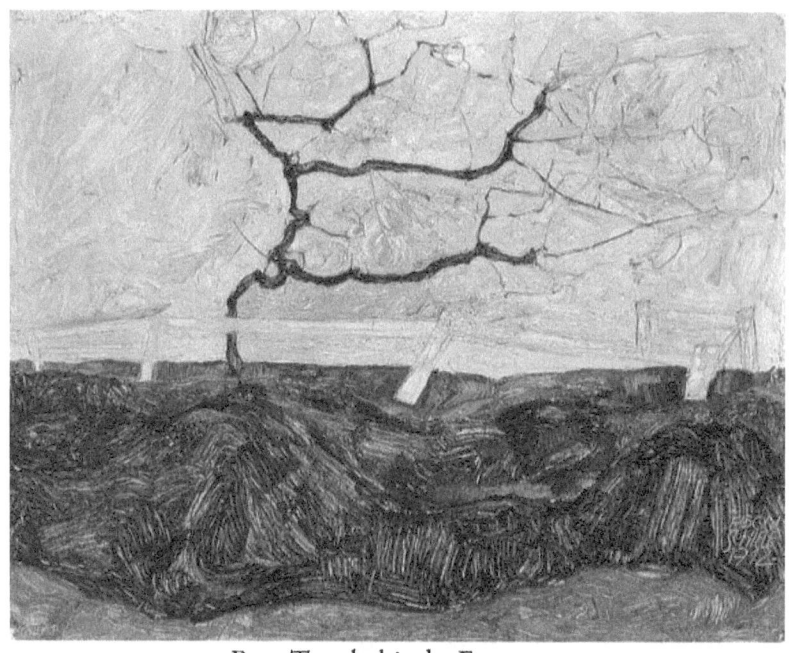

Bare Tree behind a Fence
1912, Oil on panel, Private collection

Jessica Findley

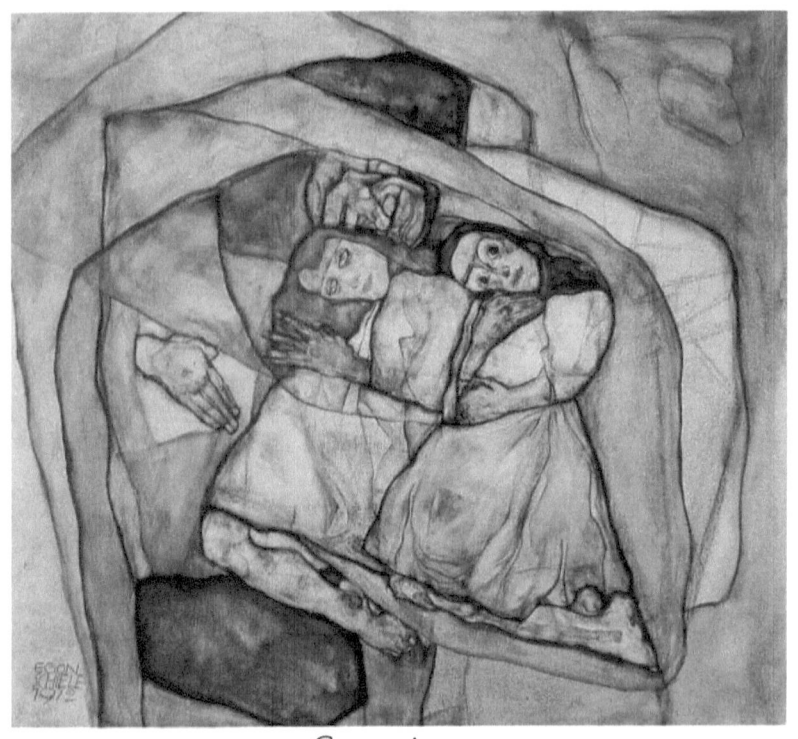

Conversion
1912, Oil on canvas, Private collection

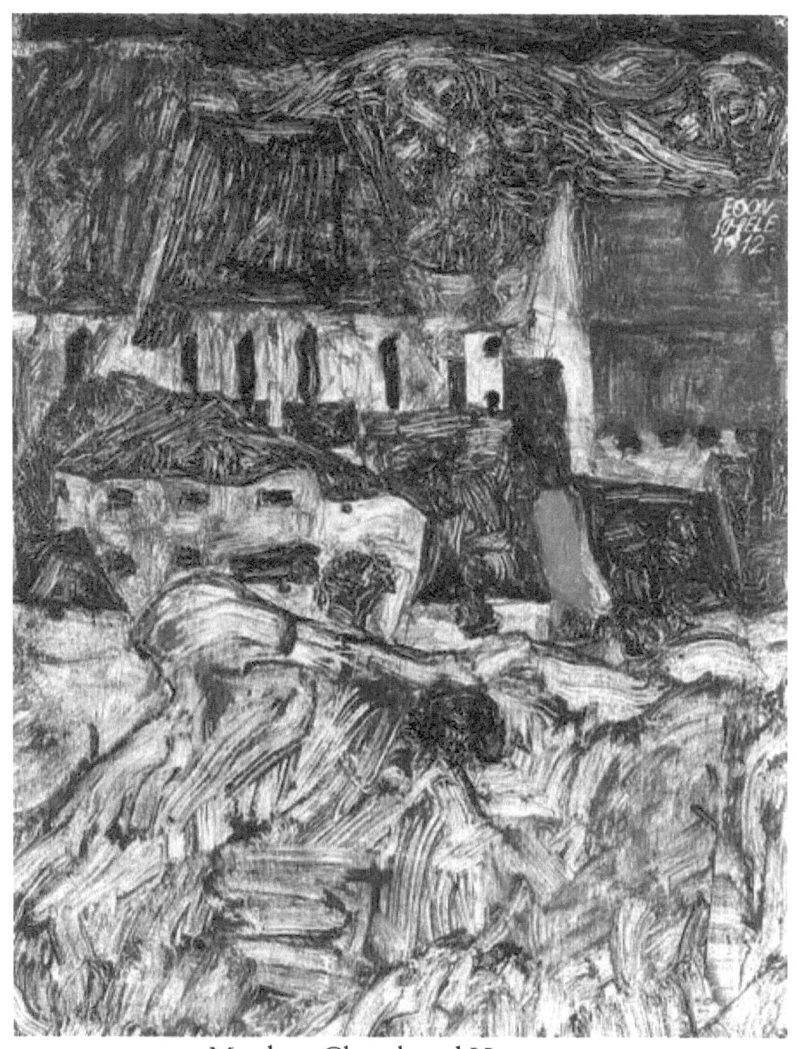

Meadow, Church and Houses
1912, Oil on panel, 36.8 x 29.2 cm, Private collection

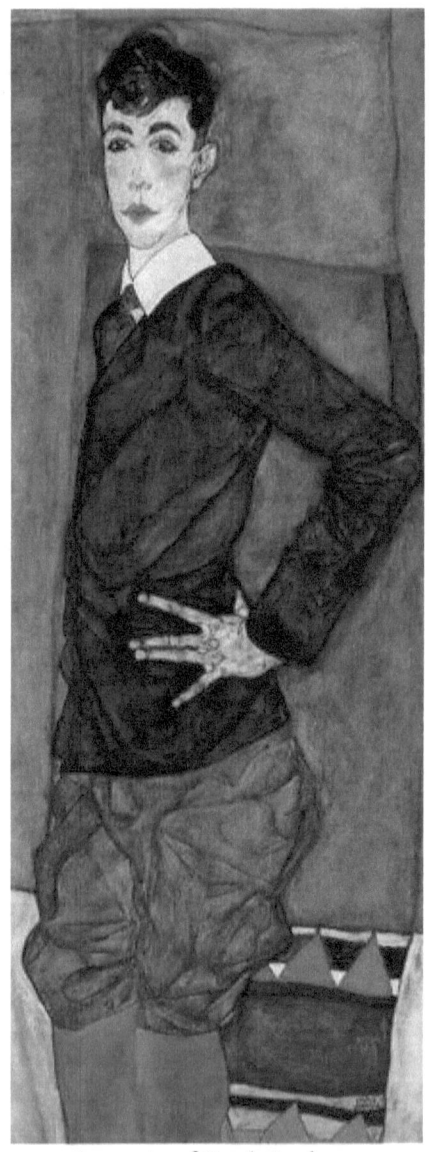

Portrait of Erich Lederer
1912, Oil on canvas, Kunstmuseum Basel (Switzerland)

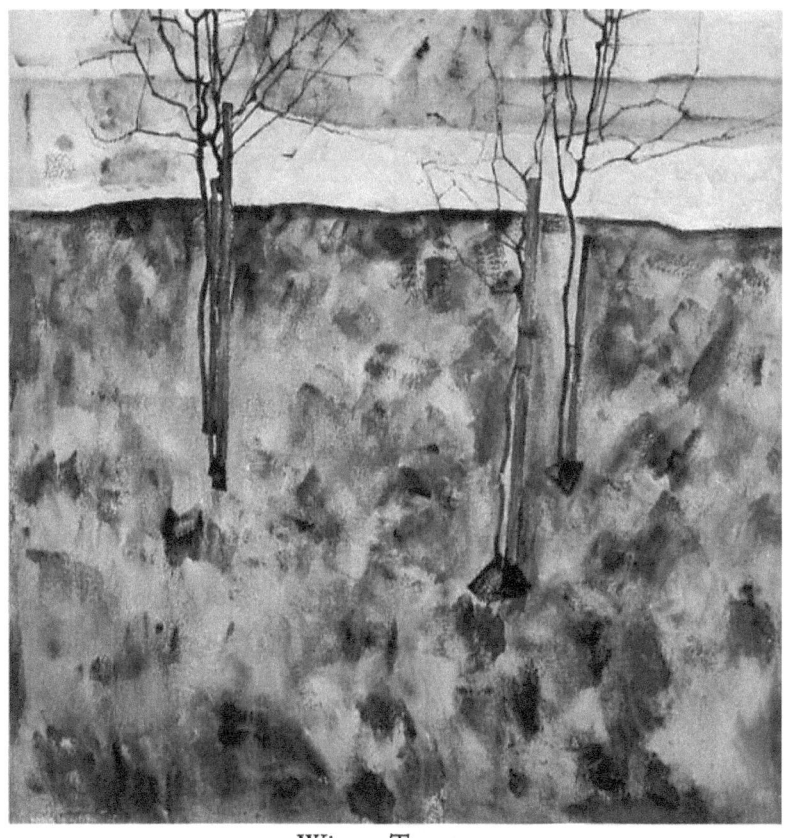

Winter Trees
1912, Oil on canvas, 80.3 x 80 cm, Private collection

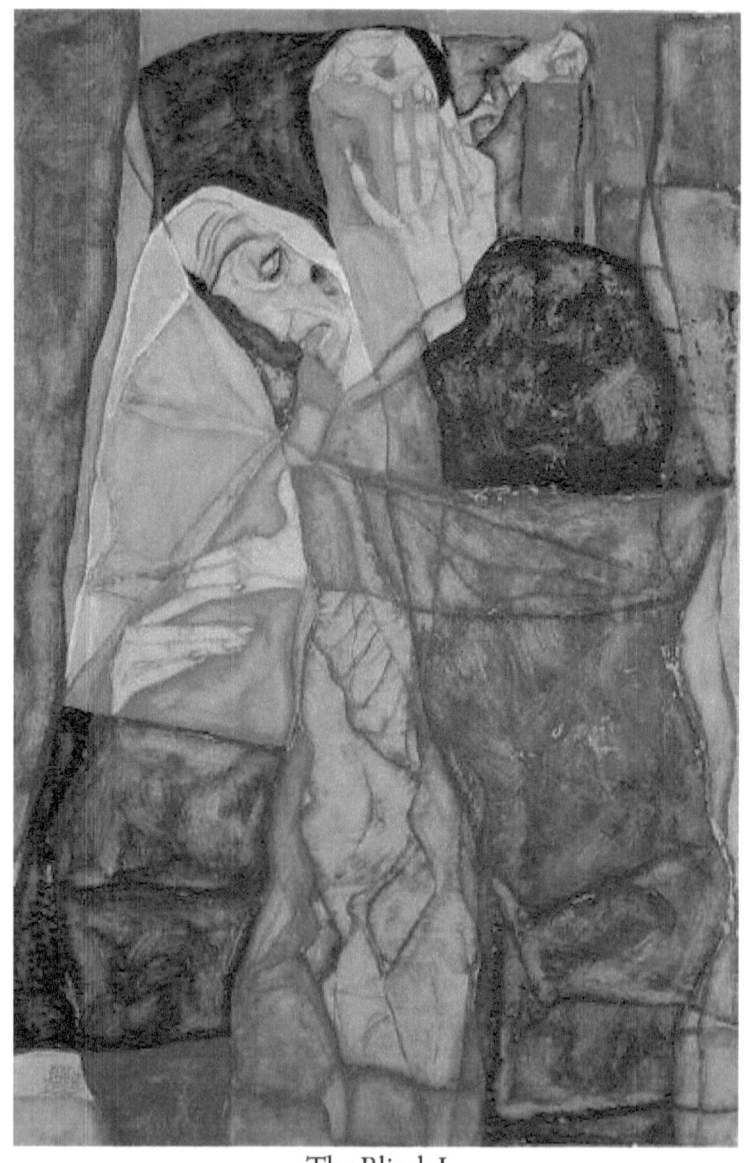

The Blind, I
1913, Oil on canvas, Private collection

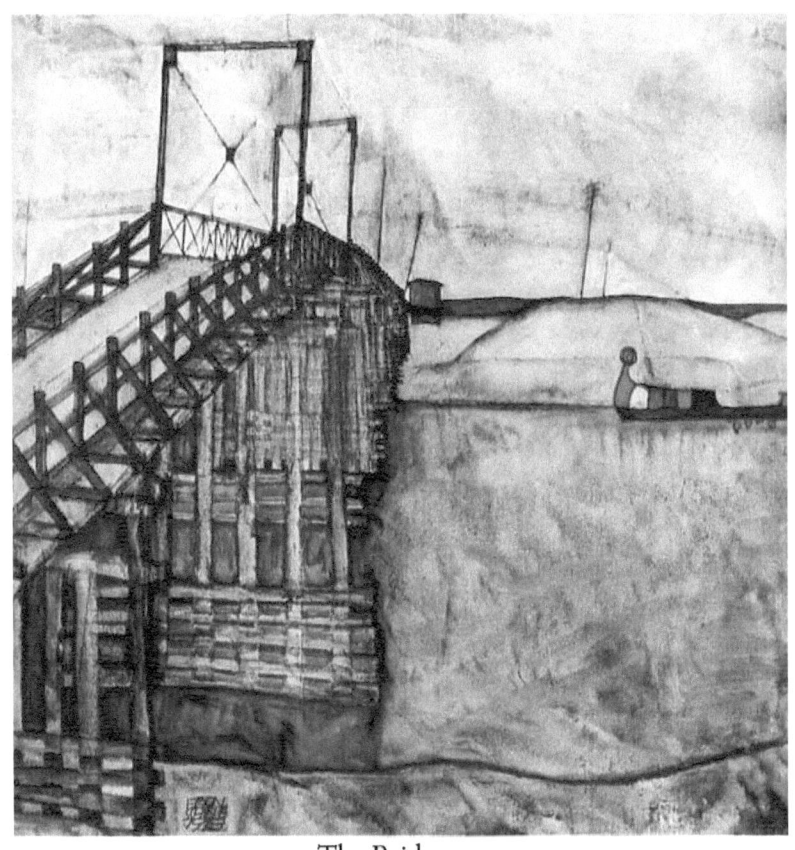

The Bridge
1913, Oil on canvas, 89.7 x 90 cm, Private collection

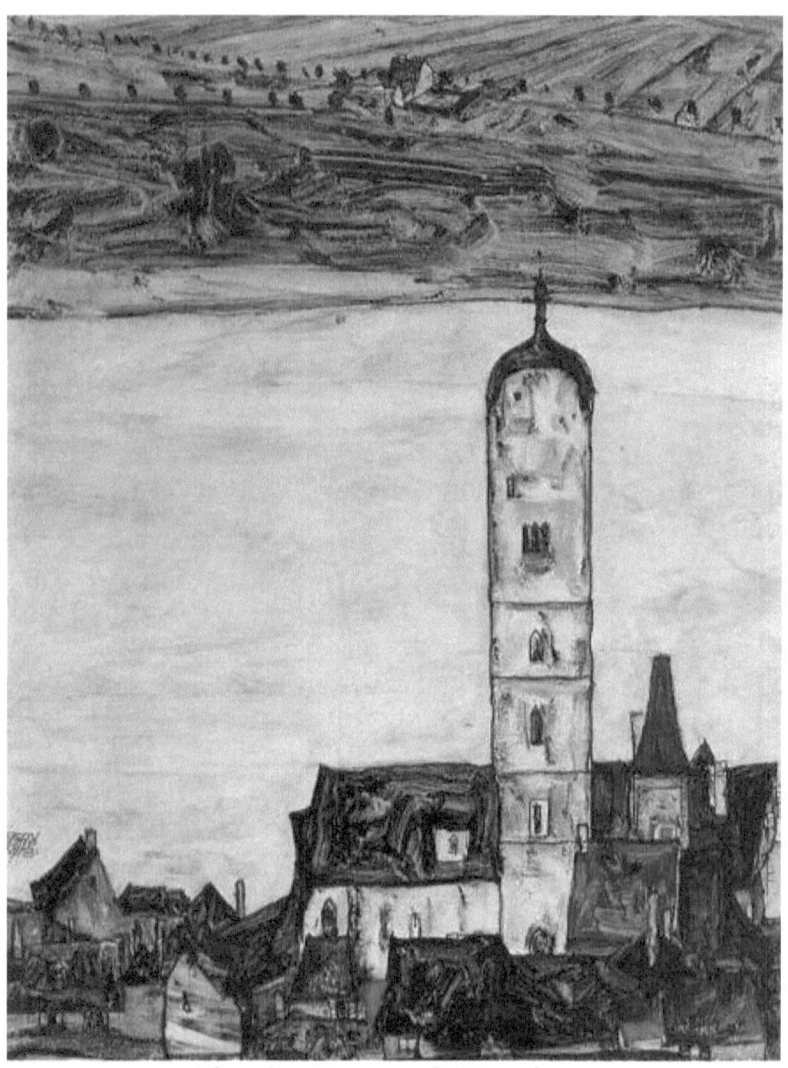

Church in Stein on the Danube
1913, Oil on panel, Private collection

EGON SCHIELE

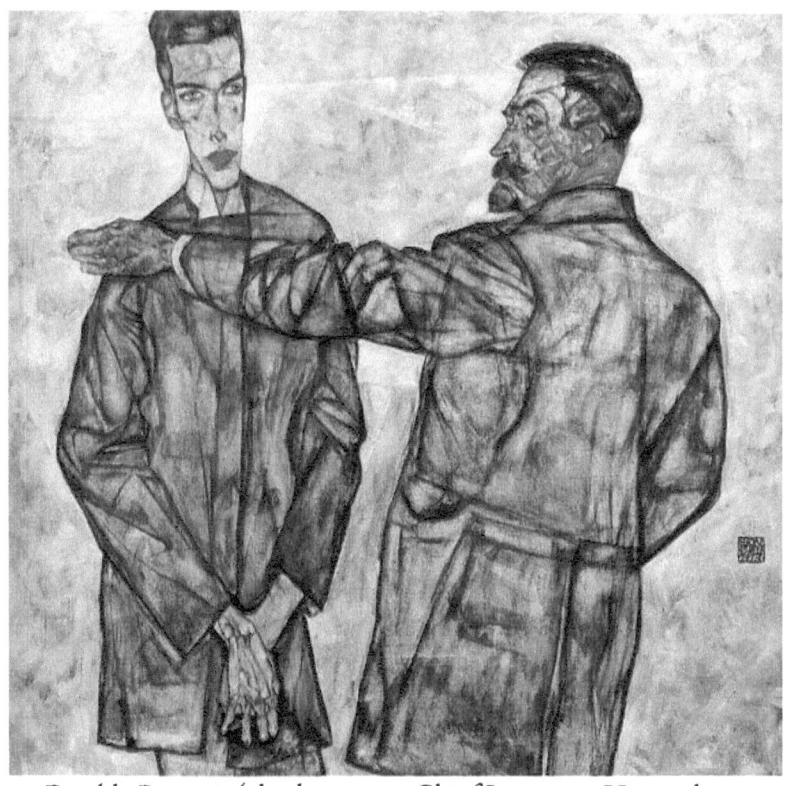

Double Portrait (also known as Chief Inspector Heinrich
Benesch and His Son Otto)
1913, Oil on canvas, 89.7 x 90 cm, Wolfgang-Gurlitt-Museum

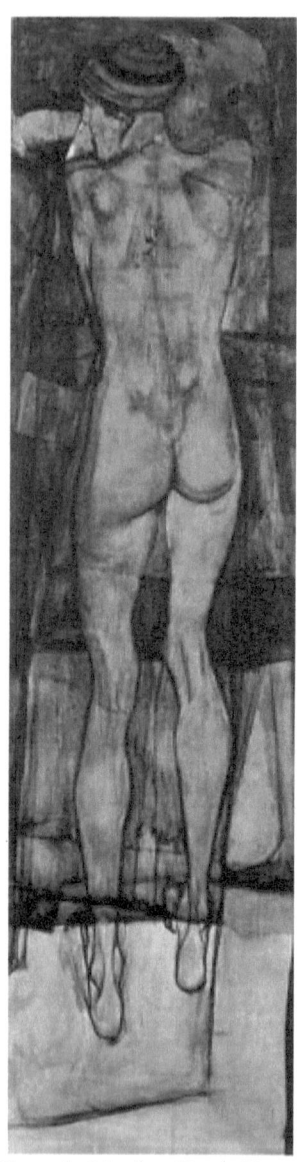

Female Nude - Back View
1913, Oil on canvas, Private collection

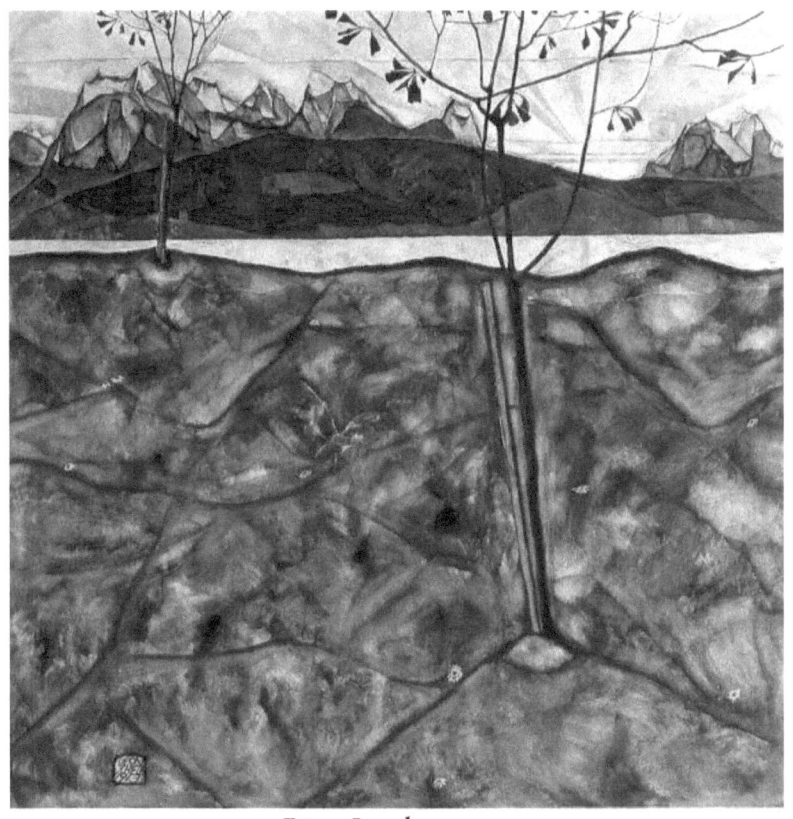

River Landscape
1913, Oil on canvas, 88.9 x 89.7 cm, Private collection

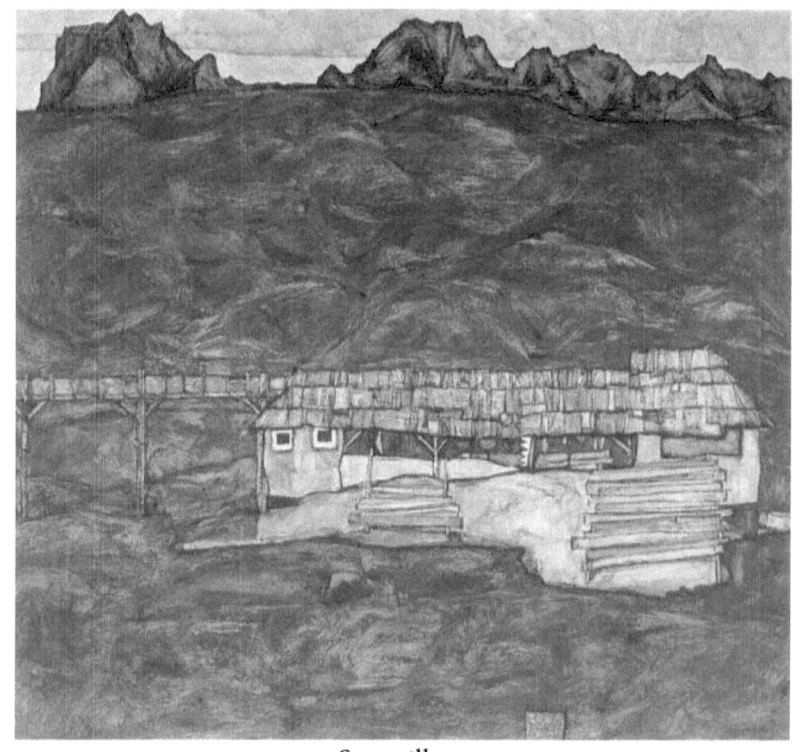

Sawmill
1913, Oil on canvas, 80.1 x 89.8 cm, Private collection

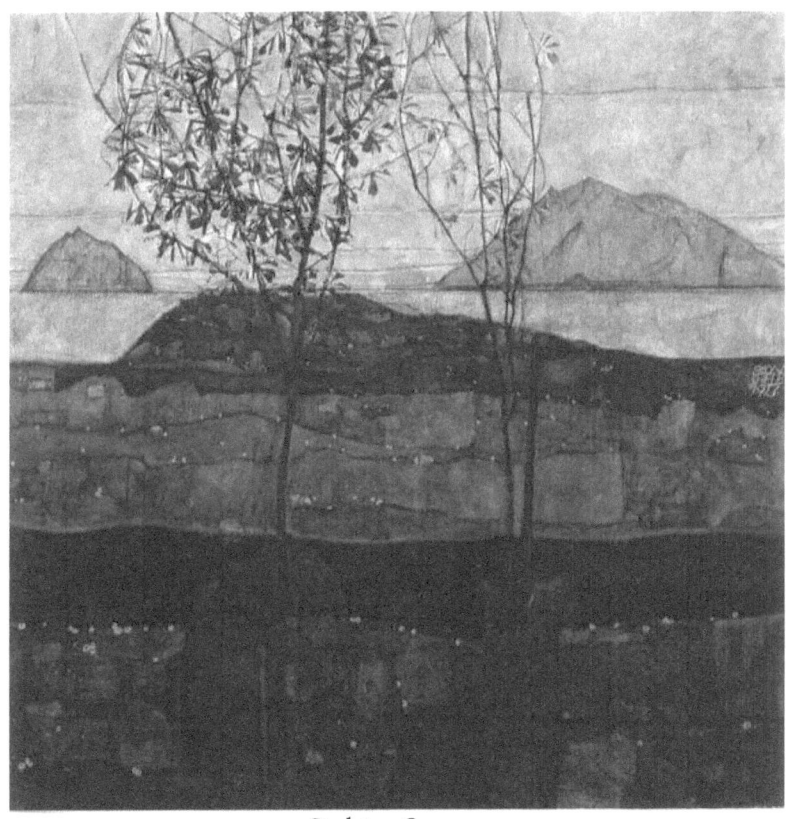

Sinking Sun
1913, Oil on canvas, 90 x 90.5 cm, Leopold Museum (Austria)
The work "Sinking Sun" is a farewell painting. The foreground is dark and infused with an infinite sense of cold, the sea is gray. The sky glows in a faint shade of carmine red. The horizontal lines are broken up by two young, almost bare trees whose dry leaves are stiffened by the cold. The sun is sinking almost imperceptibly as a small ball into the sea. It is taking its leave, and perhaps it will never return.

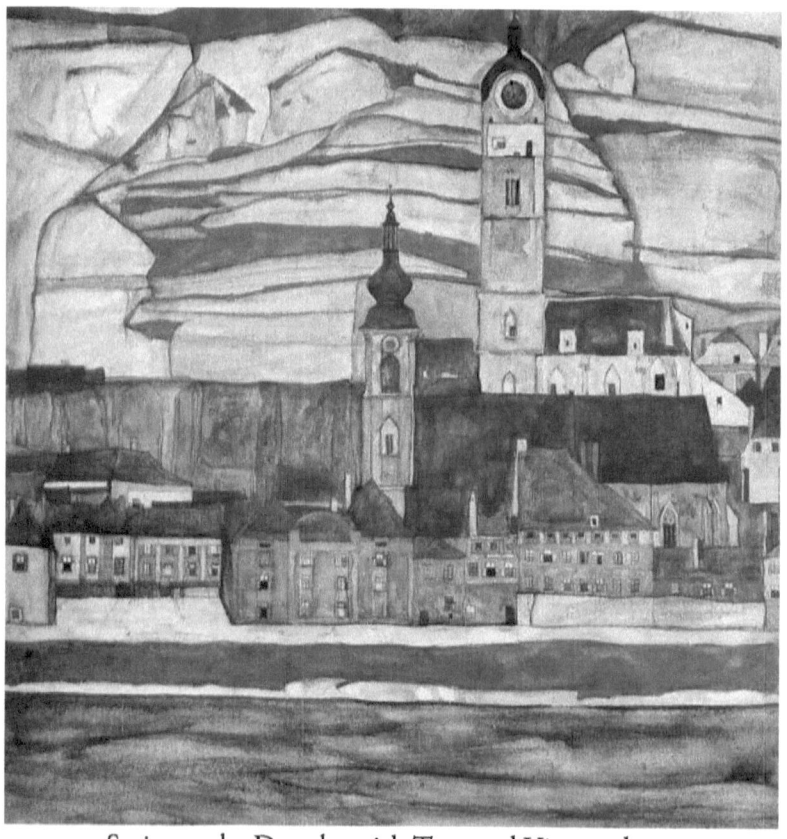

Stein on the Danube with Terraced Vineyards
1913, Oil on canvas, 89.8 x 89.6 cm, Private collection

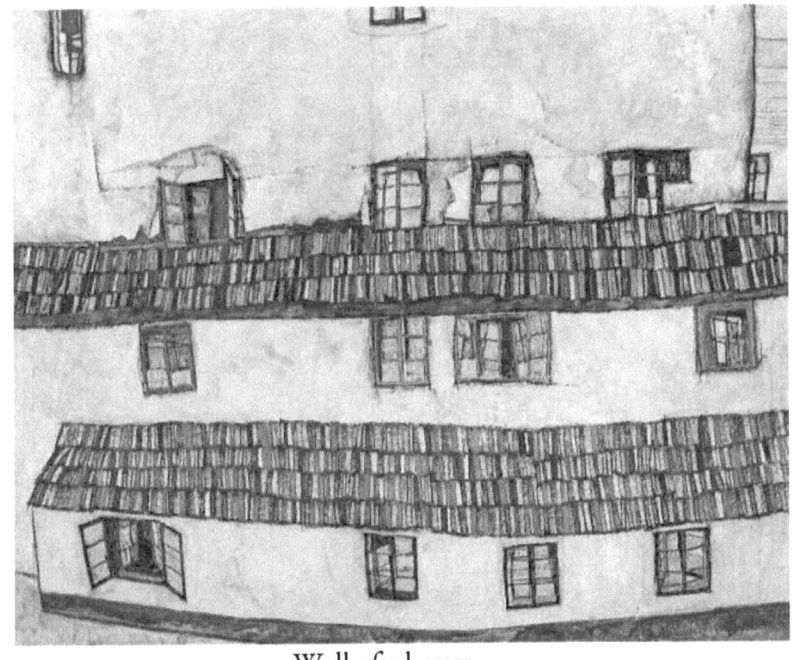

Wall of a house
1914, Oil on canvas, 110 x 140 cm, Osterreichische Galerie,
Vienna

This painting is one of the municipal views of Krumau (Czech Krumlov), Schiele's mother's place of birth in Southern Bohemia. Schiele, however, does not portray the well-known sights of this small town, but he depicts details of peripheral municipal architecture. From a high perspective, Schiele depicts a house wall parallel to the three horizontal zones of the shingle-roof borders in the picture. The house wall reaches beyond the picture borders to the left and right as well as on top. Only the bottom margin is still situated within the picture format. This partial depiction makes the observer view the objects more intensely. As opposed to the standard viewing of a picture from a distance, the detail becomes significant. By drawing the layers of the house wall parallel to the picture borders Schiele defines strange perspective. The effect of the picture is based on the contrast between the colorful windows and the white roughcast uneven wall. The windows also seem to be alive due to their irregular shapes and order and even though they are open, they do not reveal any glimpse of a human soul. All of Schielers other municipal views are also inanimate; they correspond to a type of "necropolis" (dead city), and are meant to be a metaphor of a dying, if not dead world.

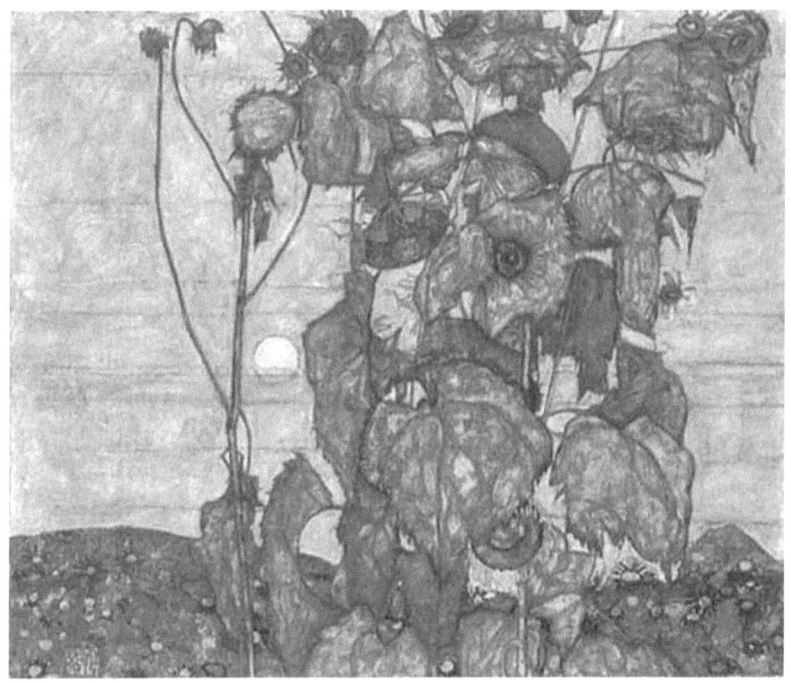

Herbstsonne (Autumn Sun)
1914, Oil on canvas, 100 x 120.5 cm, lost

Herbstsonne (Autumn Sun) is a lost masterpiece of Schiele's art unseen since 1942 and thought, until now, to have been destroyed in the Second World War. One of Schiele's most important paintings and among the finest of all his landscapes, it is the culmination of a central theme in Schiele's work that had preoccupied him since first coming to artistic maturity in 1910. Using landscape as an allegory of a human emotion, Herbstsonne is an 'Expressionist' landscape in the truest sense of the word and a masterpiece of the unique and precarious time in which it was made. Painted in March 1914 and depicting a column of sunflowers withering against a dying sunset, its overwhelming atmosphere of both melancholy and decay reflects both the natural spirit of the artist and a prescient sense that the unique and in some ways golden era to which he belonged was also coming to an end.

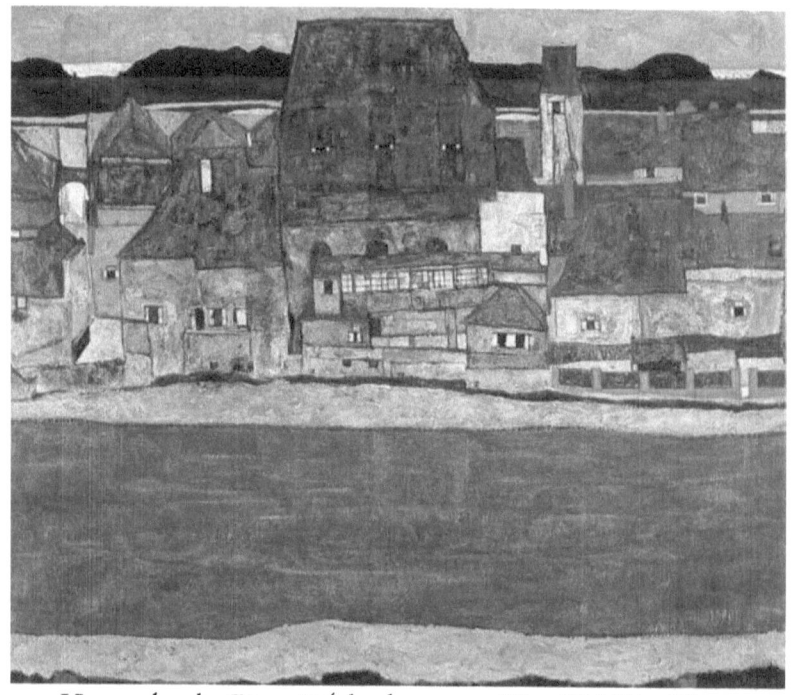

Houses by the River II (also known as The Old City II)
1914, Oil on canvas, 100 x120.5 cm, Thyssen-Bornemisza
Museum (Spain)

EGON SCHIELE

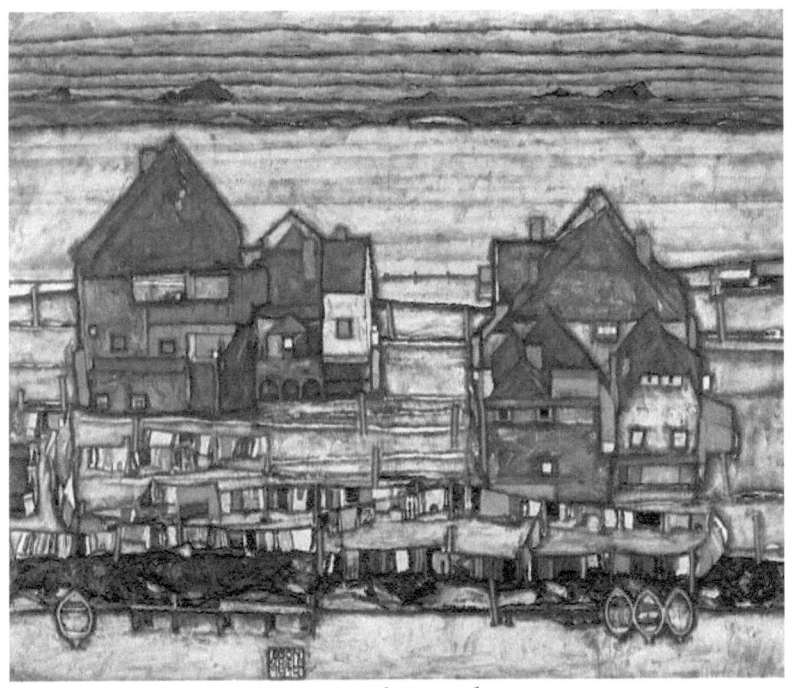

Houses with Laundry
1914, Oil on canvas, Private collection

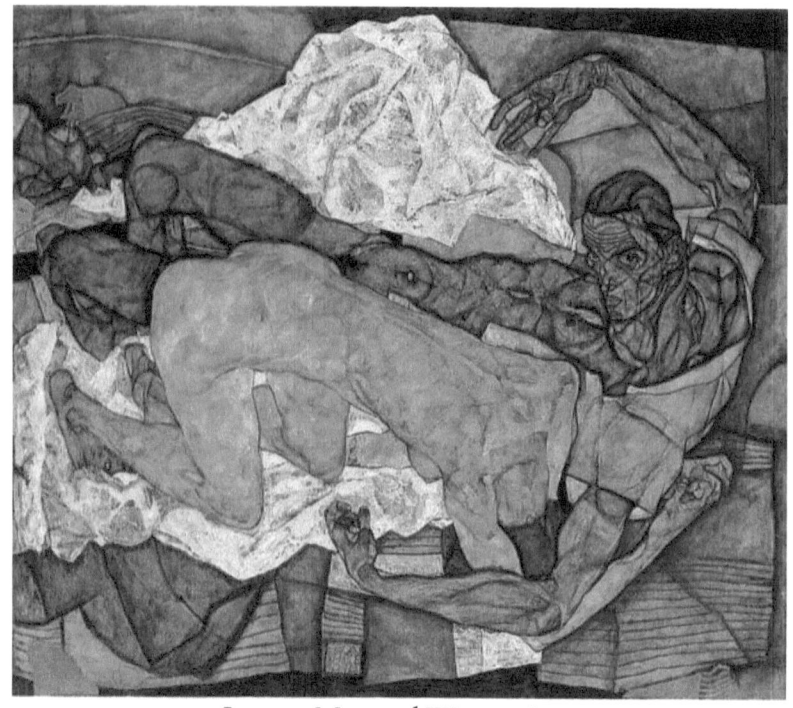

Lovers: Man and Woman I
1914, Oil on canvas, 119 x 139 cm, Private collection

EGON SCHIELE

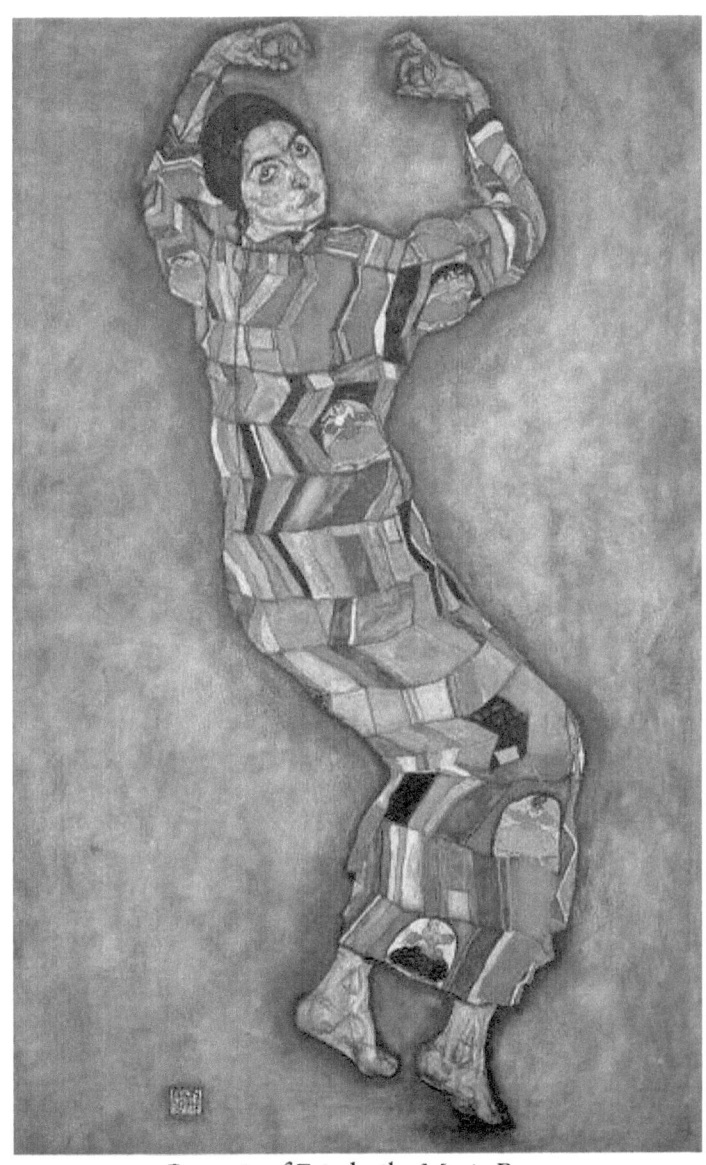

Portrait of Friederike Maria Beer
1914, Oil on canvas, Private collection

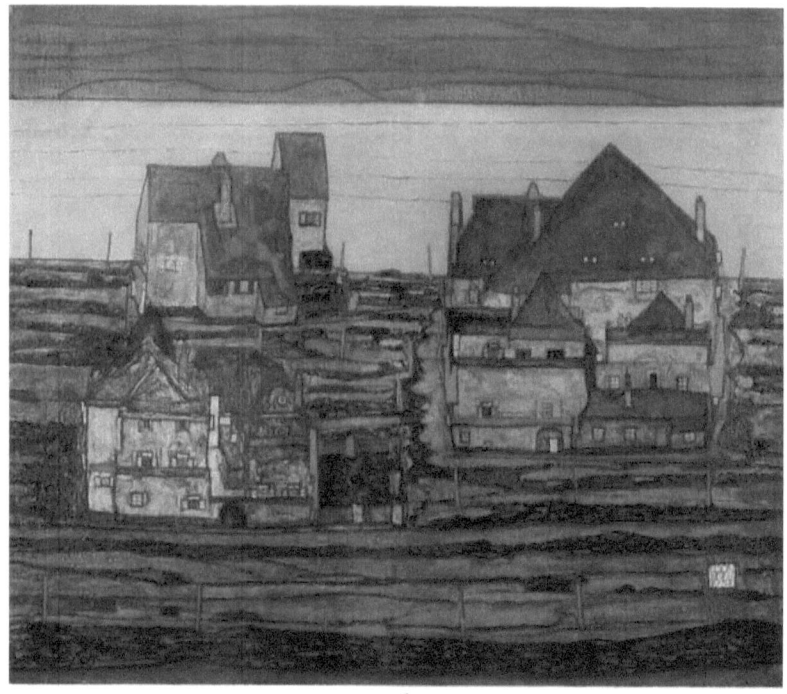

Vorstadt I
1914, Oil on canvas mounted on pressed wood, Staatsgalerie
Stuttgart (Germany)

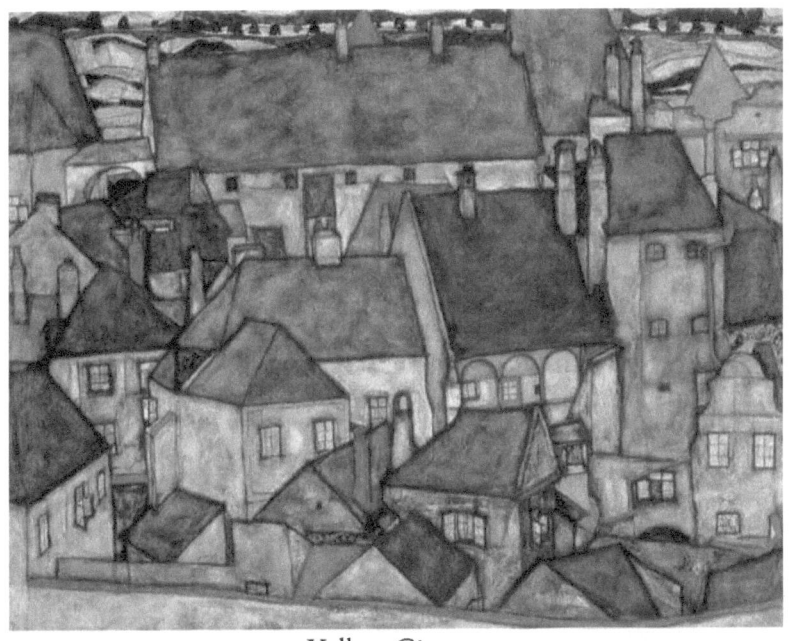

Yellow City
1914, Oil on canvas, 110 x140 cm, Private collection

Jessica Findley

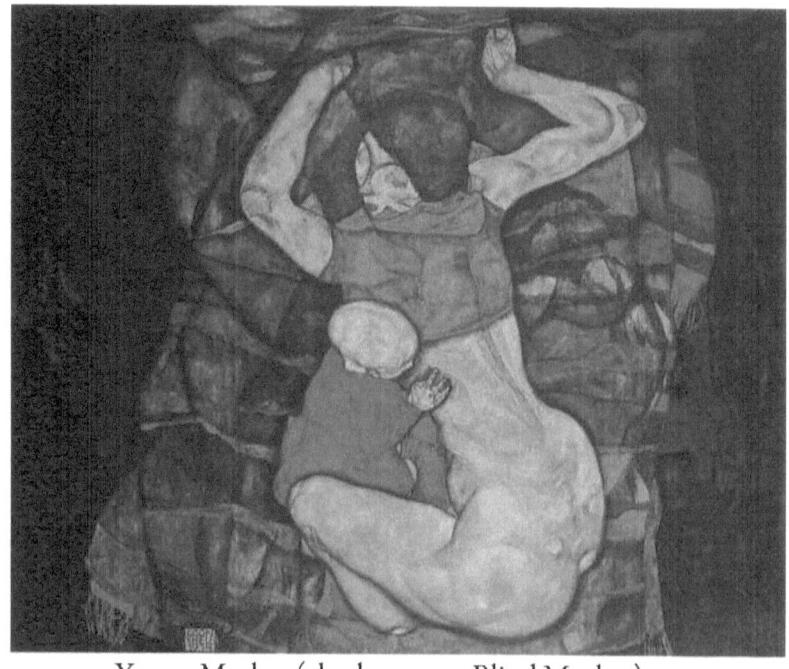

Young Mother (also known as Blind Mother)
1914, Oil on canvas, Private collection

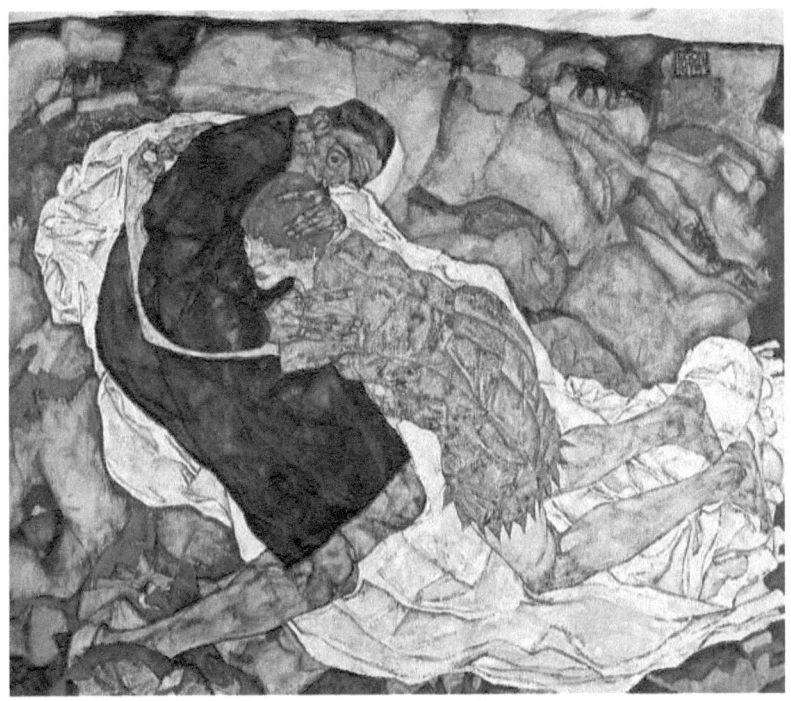

Death and the Maiden
1914–15, Oil on canvas, Osterreichische Galerie, Belvedere,
Austria

In this painting, one of Schiele's most complex and haunting works, the female figure, gaunt and tattered, clings to the male figure of death, while surrounded by an equally tattered, quasi-surreal landscape. As elsewhere in his work, in this composition Schiele combines the personal and the allegorical—in this case by turning to a theme deriving from the medieval concept of the Dance of Death that reached its height in fifteenth-century German art. Death and the Maiden was painted around the time Schiele separated from his longtime lover, Wally Neuzil, and several months before he married his new lover, Edith Harms. The painting memorializes the end of his affair with Neuzil, seemingly conveying this separation as the death of true love. Interestingly enough, the manner in which Schiele's figures are nearly consumed by their clothing and abstracted surroundings suggests the portraiture of Klimt, who likewise placed his subjects within indecipherable environments.

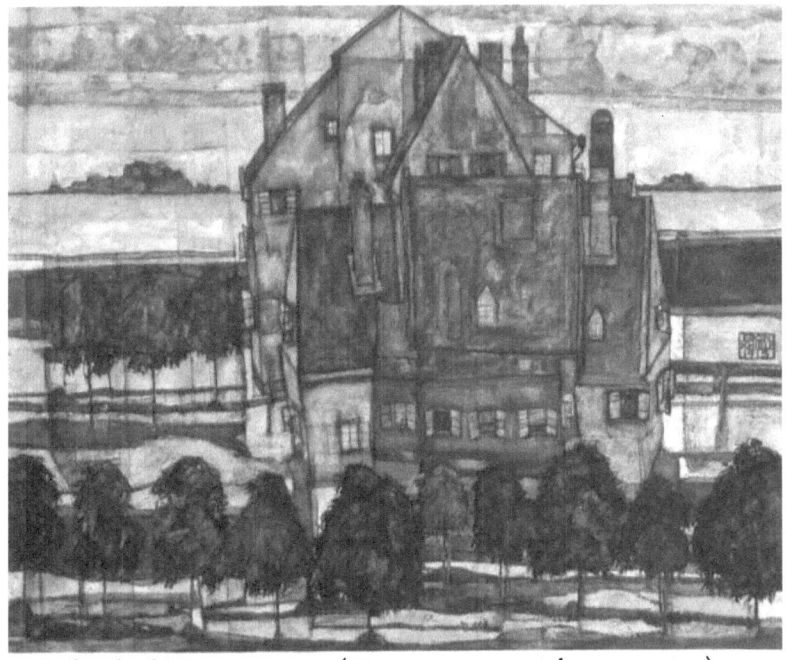

Individual House cottage (House cottage with mountains)
1915, Oil on canvas, 109.8 x 139.7 cm, Private collection

Concentrated in the center of the canvas, the buildings in Einzelne Hauser take on an almost human quality, recalling the contorted, naked bodies that fill so many of Schiele's figure oils and drawings. The houses in this 1915 painting appear to be huddled together as though for warmth, yet the skeletal angularity of these structures hints at a singular lack of solace or shelter. Schiele's landscapes, especially from the period of 1912 onwards - the years of his full expressionistic maturity - involve a strange and heady mixture of his own deeply personal references, his sparingly modern style and the projection of emotions upon the scene before him.

Jessica Findley

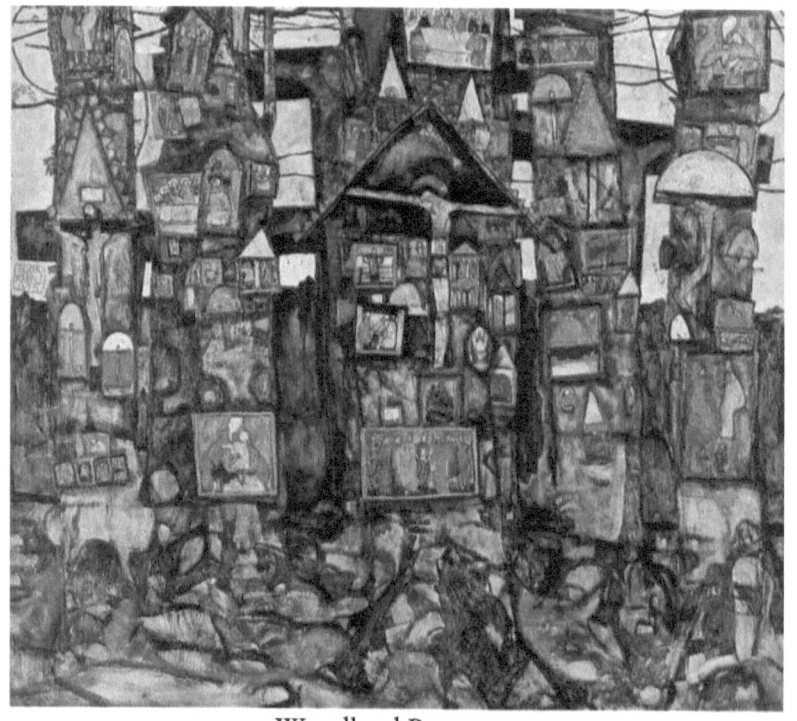

Woodland Prayer
1915, Oil on canvas, Private collection

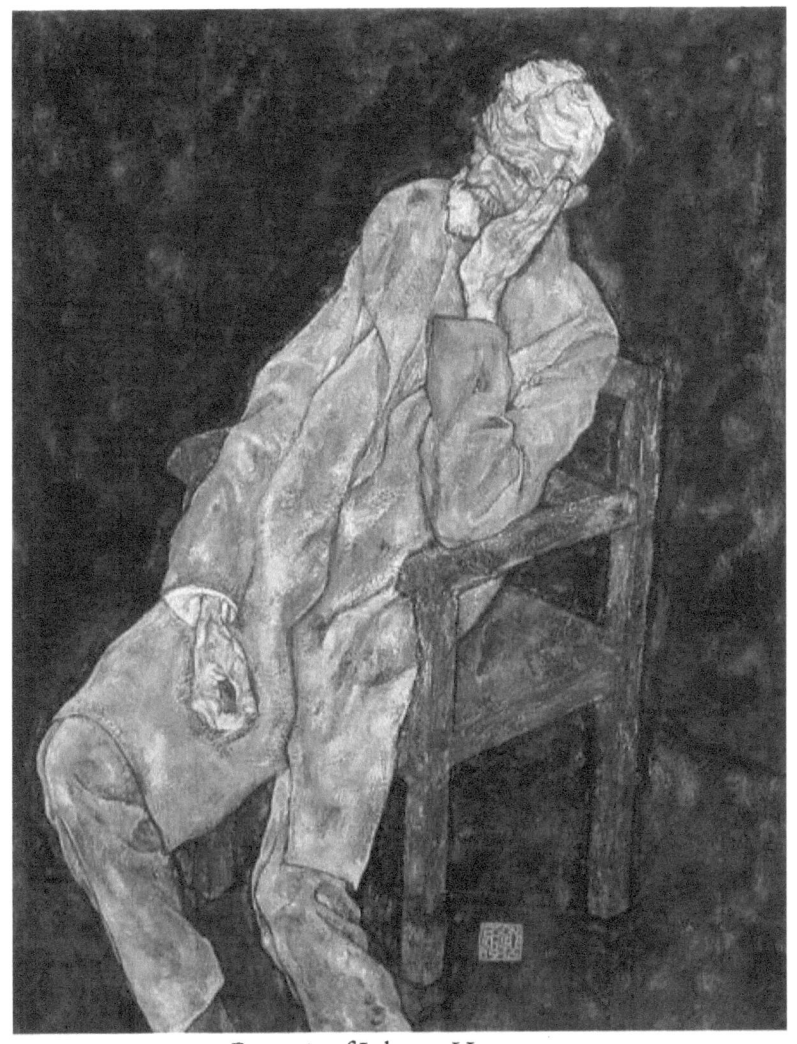

Portrait of Johann Harms
1916. Oil with wax on canvas, 141 x 110.8 cm, Solomon R.
Guggenheim Museum, New York

The subject of Egon Schiele's portrait is Johann Harms, his father-in-law. The painting demonstrates Schiele's sympathy for the 73-year-old man, a retired machinist with the Austrian railway. Although a family portrait, it conveys a somber monumentality. With a stateliness that transcends its subject, the painting is reminiscent of papal portraits by Raphael or Titian. The work is known as the first in a series of "painterly portraits," as opposed to earlier canvases that Schiele executed in a more graphic style.

Schiele designed the chair in the painting for his studio and used it several times for portraits. As a prop, it allowed the artist to push his subjects toward the picture plane, flattening and enlarging the contours of their bodies. The chair also recalls the furniture in Vincent van Gogh's paintings of his own bedroom; its handcrafted style reminds us of the importance of the decorative arts in Vienna at this time.

Schiele painted the portrait two years before his death from influenza. It is an example of his mature style and goes far in abolishing fixed notions of Austrian Expressionism as only an art of angst. It also demonstrates that Schiele could successfully depart from his well-known fascination with the physical and psychic dimensions of sexuality. In 1916, after initial difficulties in his marriage to Edith Harms, Schiele was beginning to enjoy a sense of domestic happiness that would lead to other intimate family portraits. Schiele's fondness for Johann Harms carried beyond this portrait—after the old man's death in 1917, Schiele made a death mask of his father-in-law.

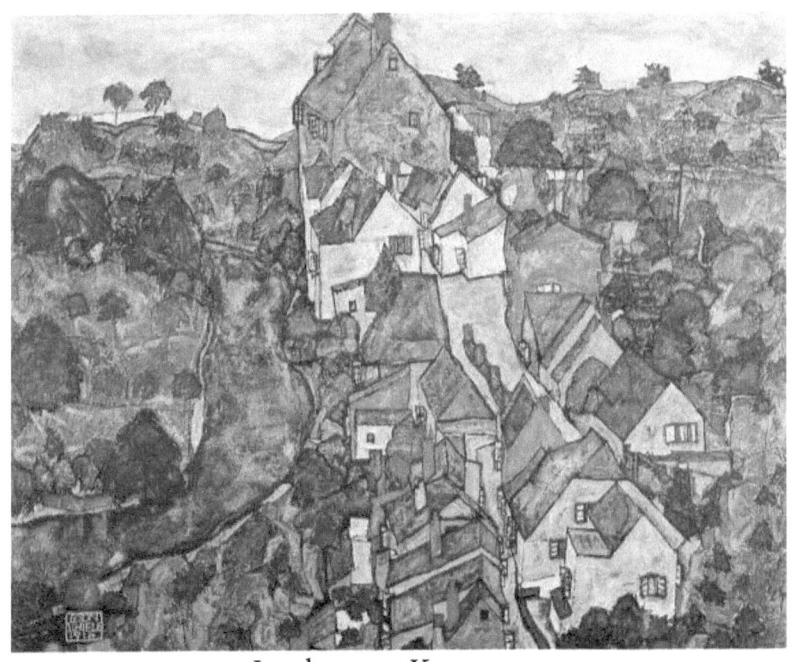

Landscape at Krumau
1916, Oil on canvas, Wolfgang-Gurlitt-Museum

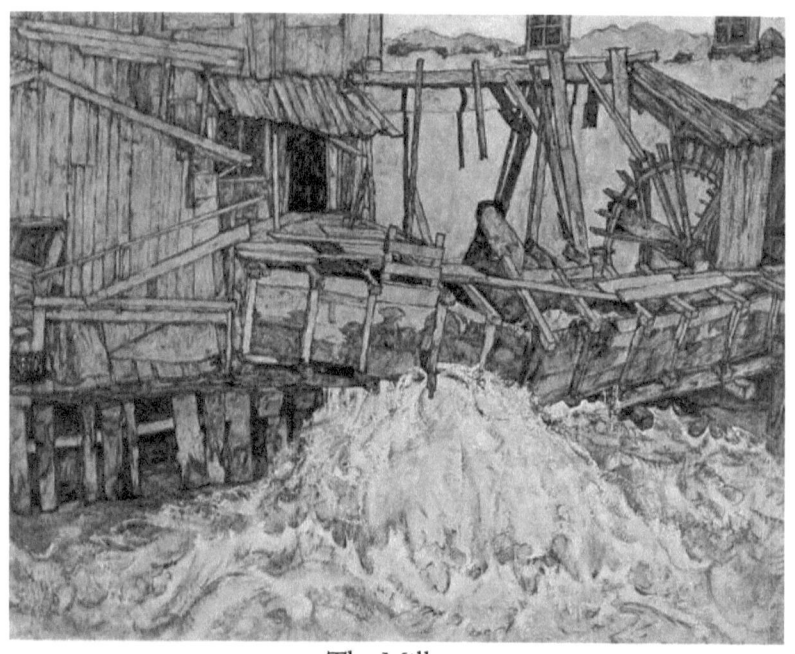

The Mill
1916, Oil on canvas, Niedersaechsisches Landesmuseum
(Germany)

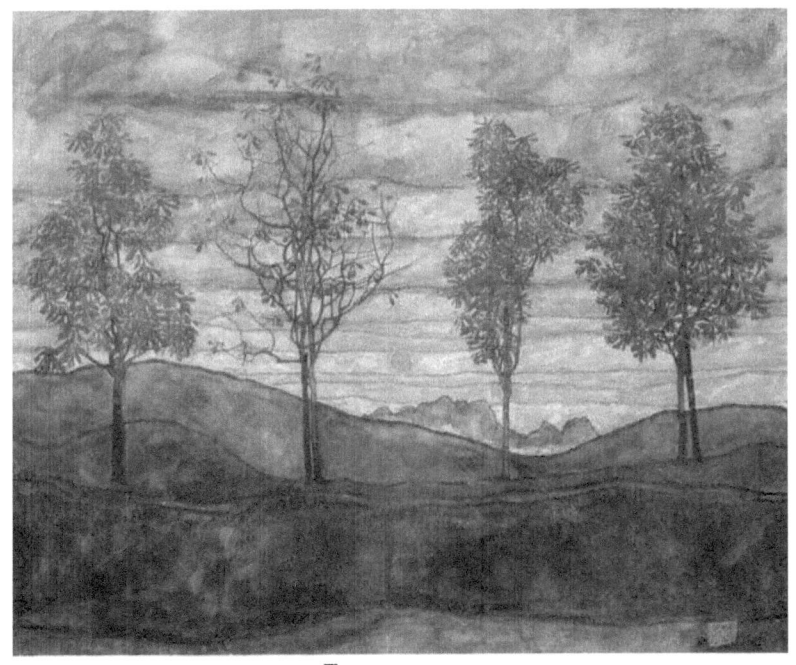

Four trees
1917, Oil on canvas, 110.5 x 141 cm, Private collection

This painting shows an unspectacular part of nature. Four chestnut trees are shown in strict geometric order and regularity. As opposed to realistic description of botanic details the arrangement of the rest of the picture results into a very scarce description of landscape. As in classic landscape painting the horizontal line of the picture can be found in the centre whereby we are given an illusion of spaciousness. Vertical to the dimension of depth there are a few levels that are parallel to the picture - as in a scenic view. On one of these levels we see the line of trees. Through this, a sharp contrast between area and space is formed.

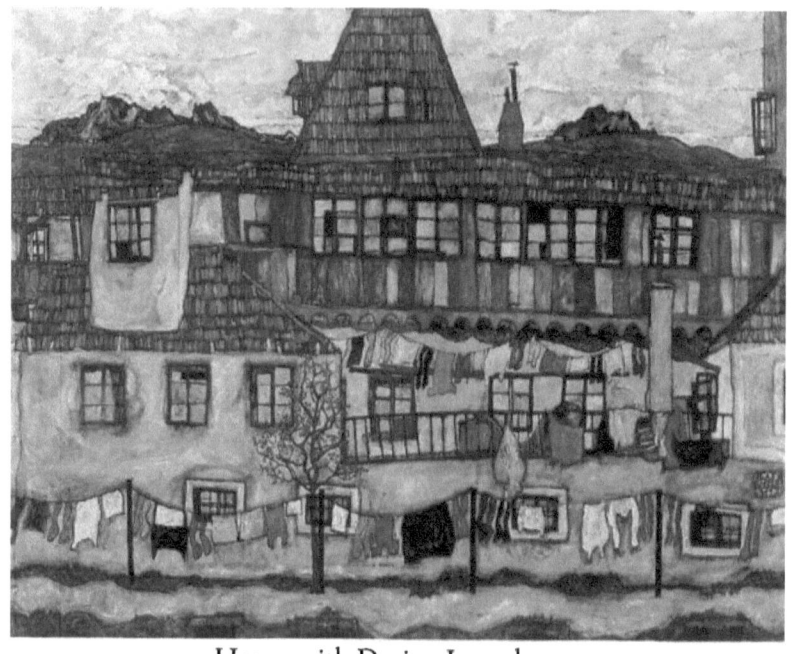

House with Drying Laundry
1917, Oil on canvas, Private collection

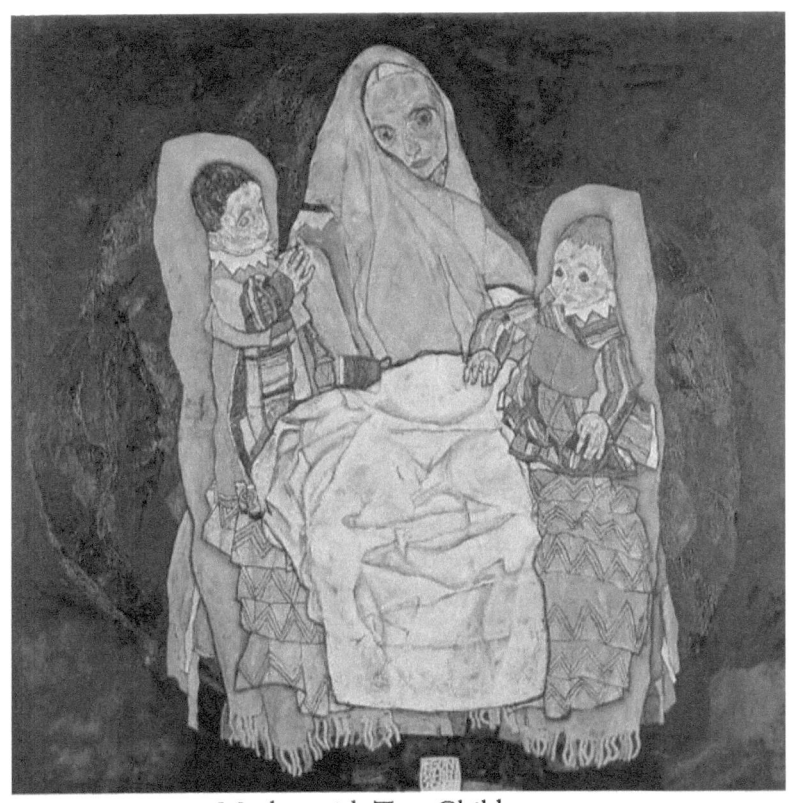

Mother with Two Children
1917, Oil on canvas, Osterreichische Galerie Belvedere
(Austria)

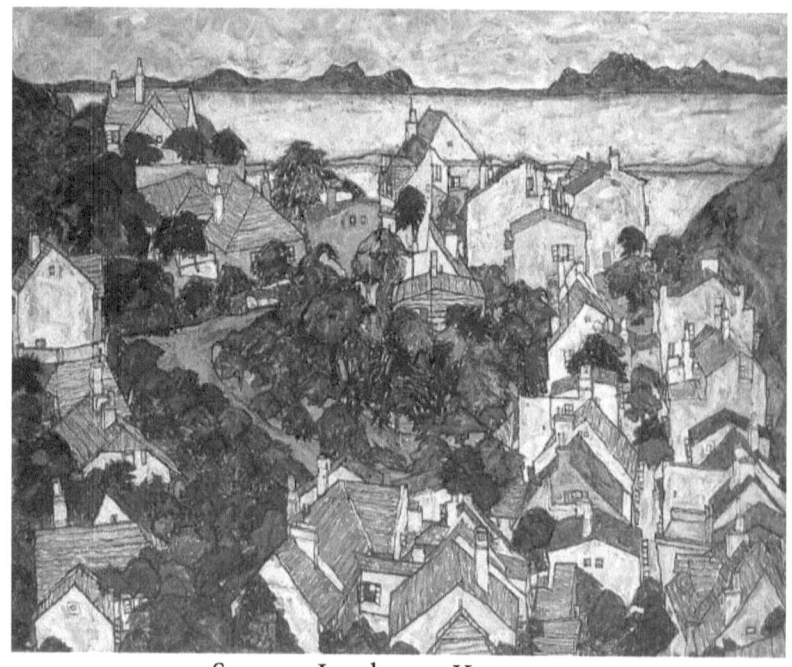

Summer Landscape, Krumau
1917, Oil on canvas, Private collection

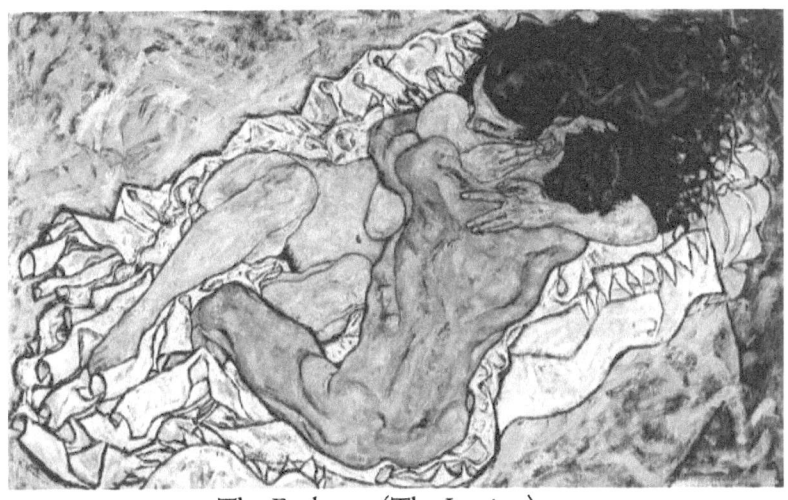

The Embrace (The Loving)
1917, Oil on canvas, O100 x 170 cm, Osterreichische Galerie
Belvedere

The original painting of "Embrace" was done by oil paint on canvas. Schiele's use of color in this piece is limited to four main shades: yellow, brown, white, and flesh tones. The design of the piece is structured in a way that focuses the viewer on the diagonal. The bodies of the man and woman lie in a diagonal line furthered by the way the woman's hair rests and the downward diagonal of the lines of the white cloth underneath them that run from right to left. The way the white cloth gathers in the lower left hand corner also emphasizes this diagonal line that runs through the entirety of the piece from the top right corner to the bottom left.

"Embrace" is characterized by flat geometric shapes, emphasized by dark, heavy outlining in black and blue paint. The figures appear to be more two dimensional than three dimensional because of this outlining. There is no roundedness to the woman or man's torso and no shadowing to give dimension to the body parts. The layers of the white cloth in the bottom right are distinguished by zigzag lines, sine curve lines, and triangles. It is only in the lower left side of the piece where we see more cylindrical shapes forming, but still with the heavy outlining, the picture is distinctly two-dimensional.

The human bodies themselves are a distorted view of reality. In general, the outline of the man's body, especially, though seen in the woman's body as well, is rather shaky and abnormally uneven. This gives an unnatural quality to the bodies, making the man seems bony at the knees and elbows despite his supposed muscular build. The body shapes as a whole are also rather elongated.

All of these characteristics are elements of Expressionism, which Schiele came to implement and master up until his early death at the age of 28.

EGON SCHIELE

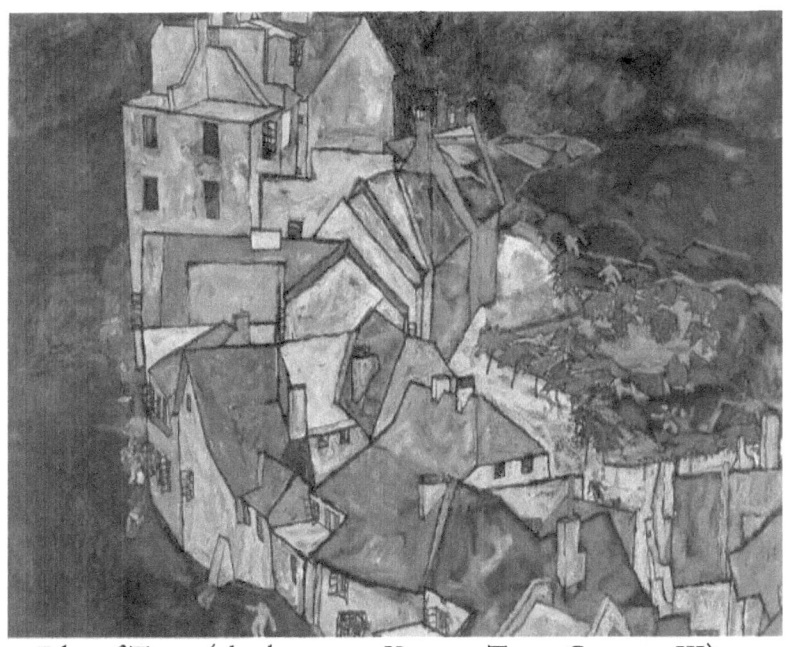

Edge of Town (also known as Krumau Town Crescent III)
1918, Oil on canvas, O109.5 x139.5 cm, Neue Galerie am
Landesmuseum (Austria)

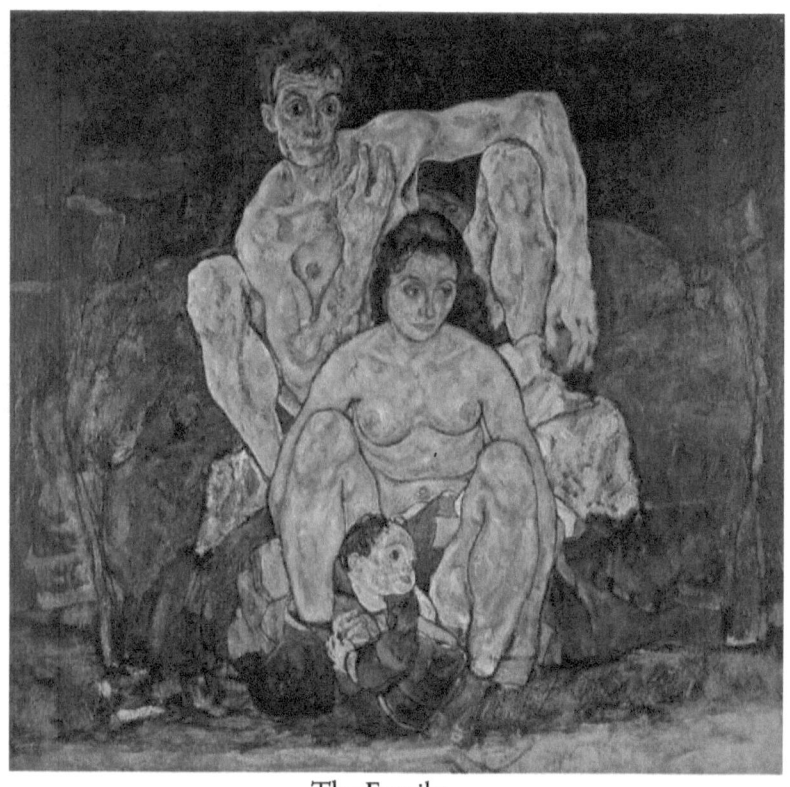

The Family
1918, Oil on canvas, 191.8 cm x 152.5 cm, Osterreichische
Galerie Belvedere

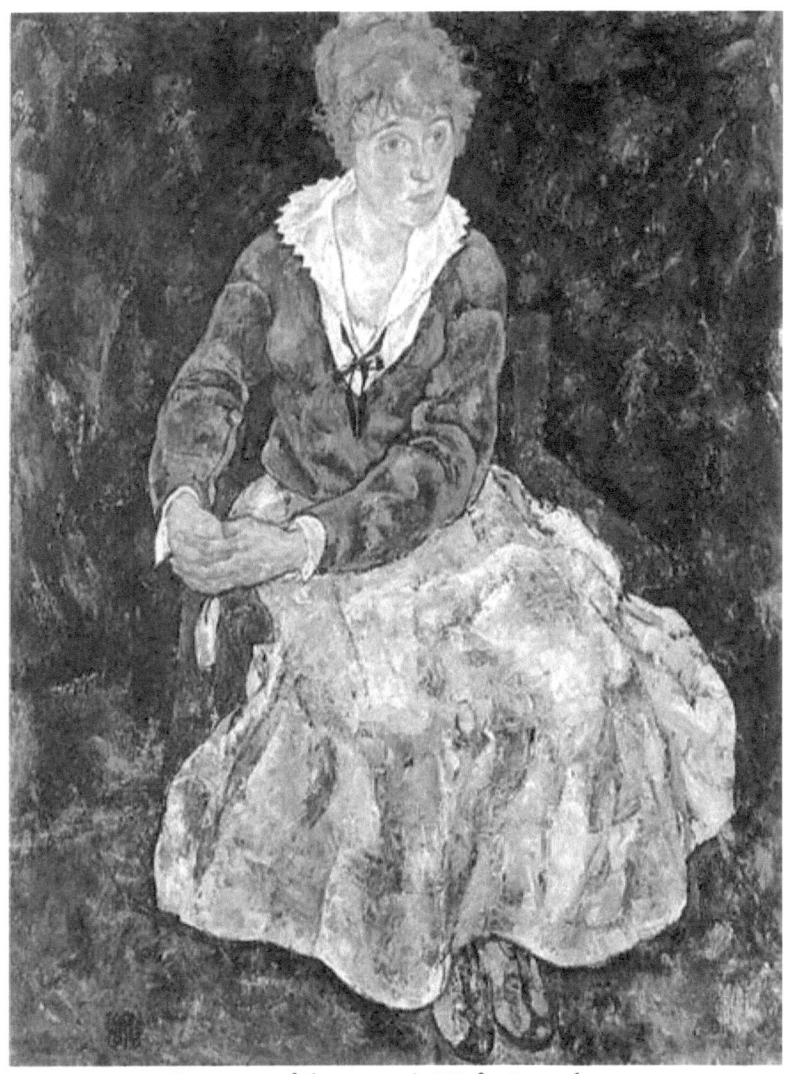

Portrait of the Artist's Wife, Seated
1918, Oil on canvas, 140 x 110 cm, Osterreichische Galerie
Belvedere

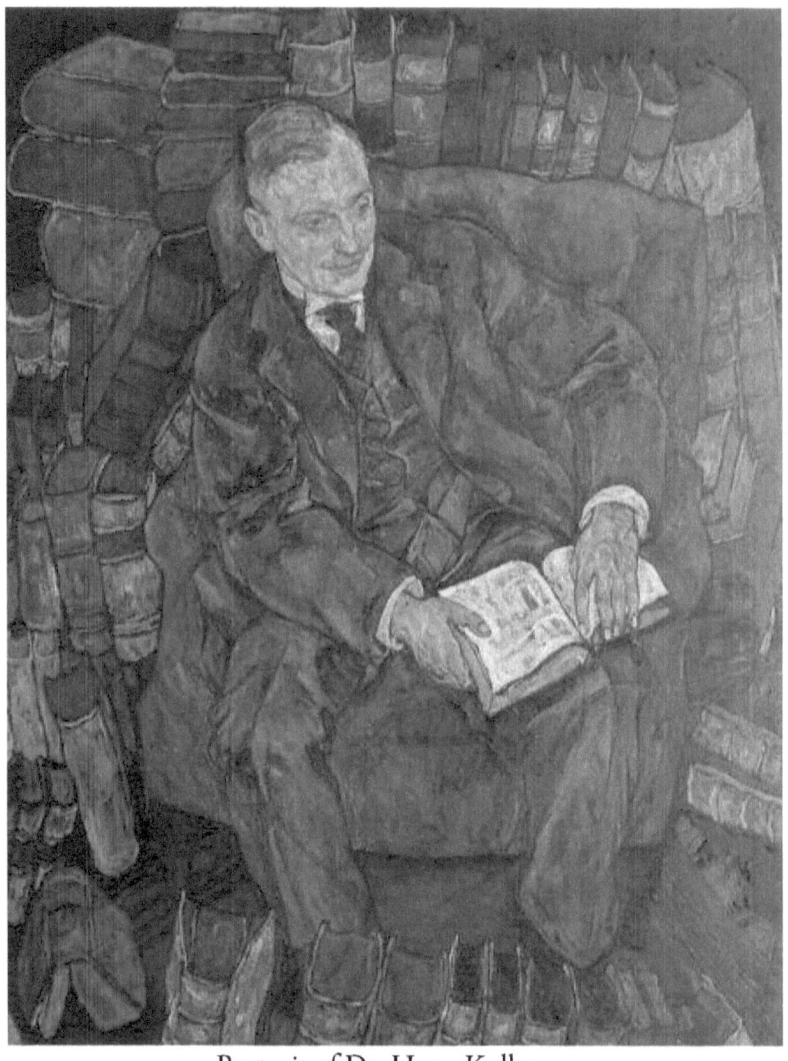

Portrait of Dr. Hugo Koller
1918, Oil on canvas, Osterreichische Galerie Belvedere

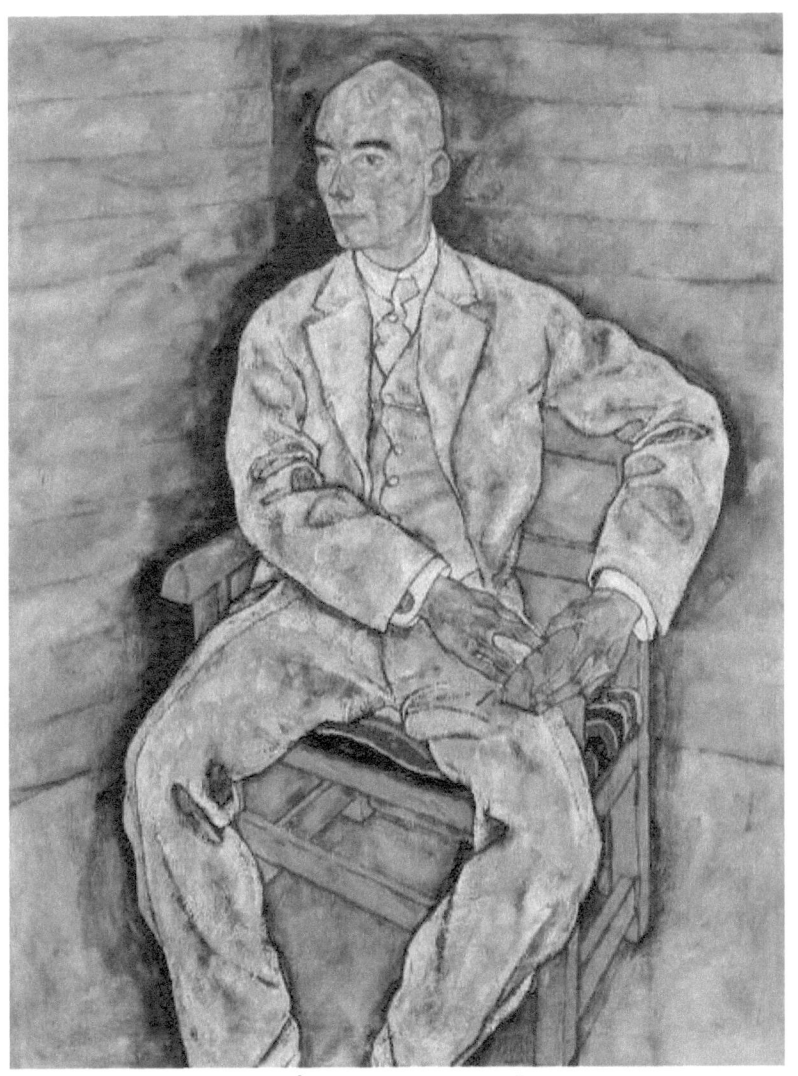

Portrait of Victor Ritter von Bauer
1918, Oil on canvas, Osterreichische Galerie Belvedere

Drawings

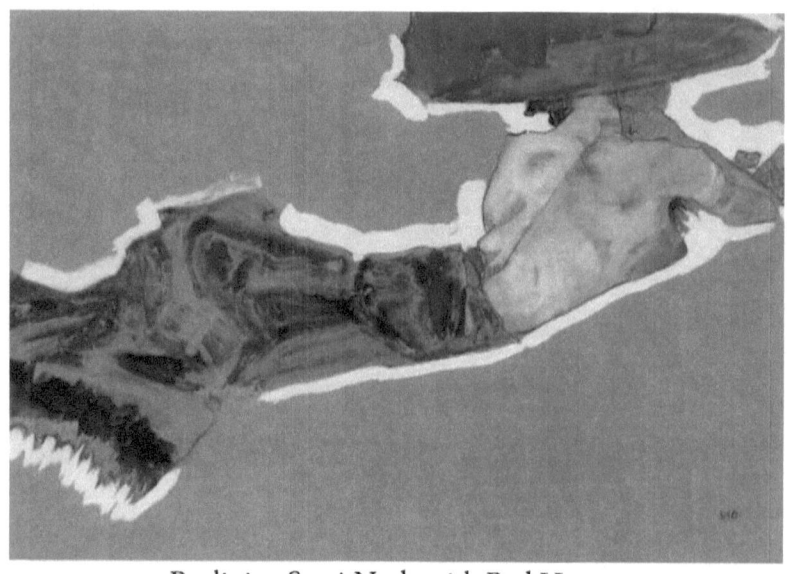

Reclining Semi-Nude with Red Hat
1910, Gouache, watercolor and crayon with white heightening,
Private collection

EGON SCHIELE

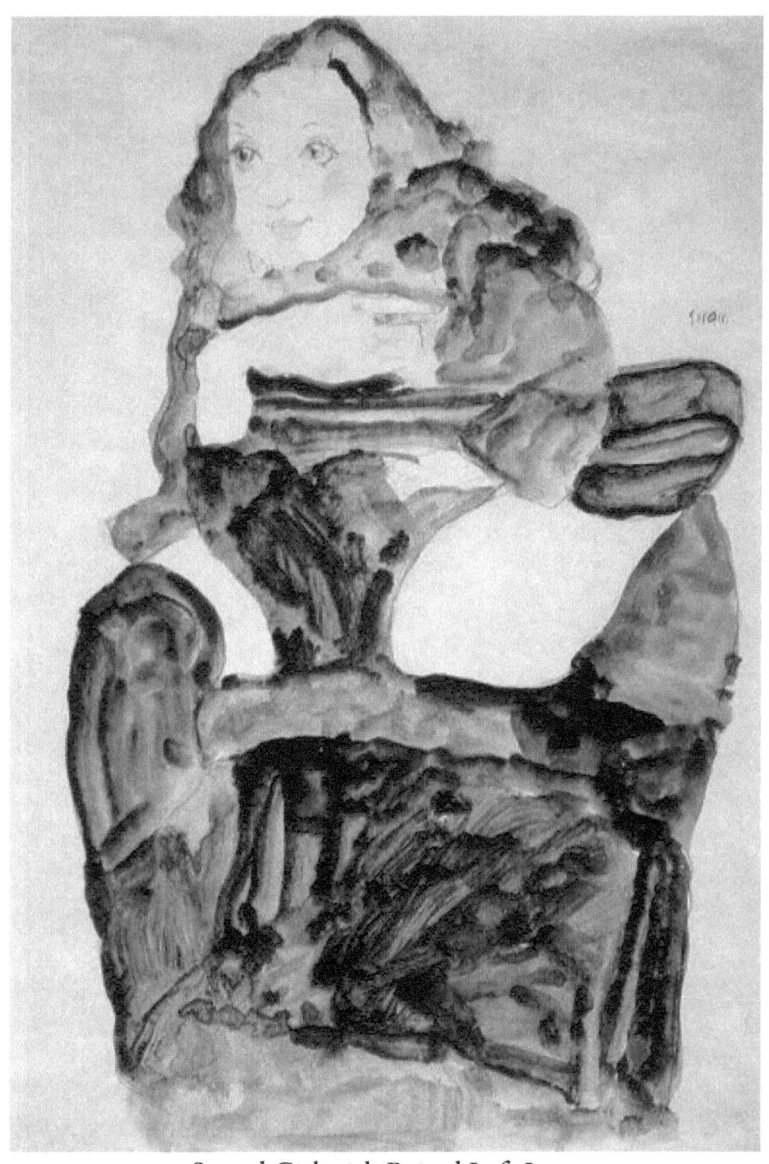

Seated Girl with Raised Left Leg
1911, Gouache, watercolor and pencil on paper, Private
collection

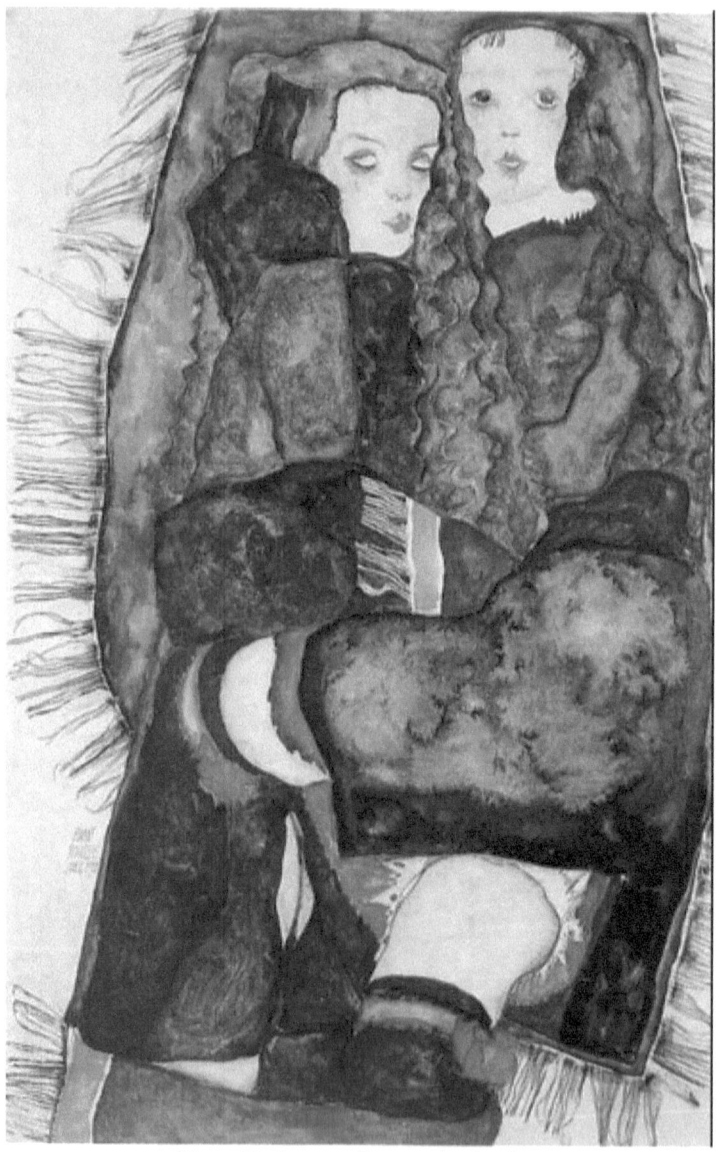

Two Girls on a Fringed Blanket
1911, Gouache, watercolor gouache, watercolor and pencil on
paper, 55.9 cm x 36.8 cm, Private collection

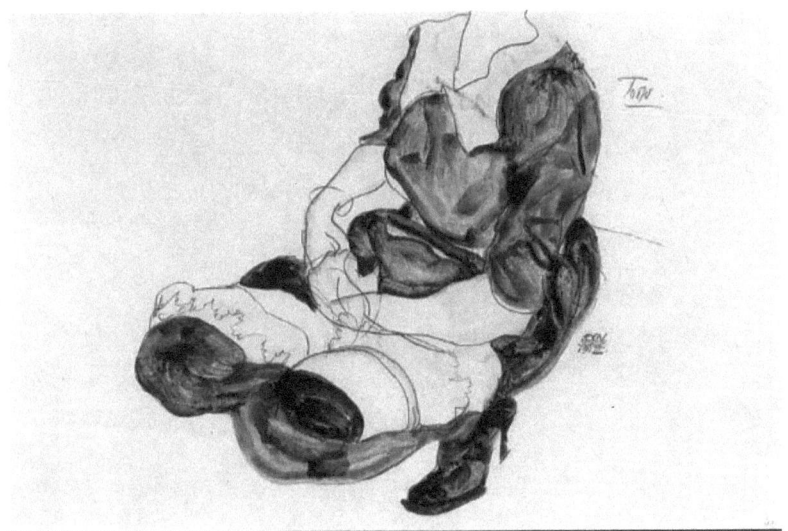

Female Torso, Squatting
1912, Watercolor and pencil on paper, Private collection

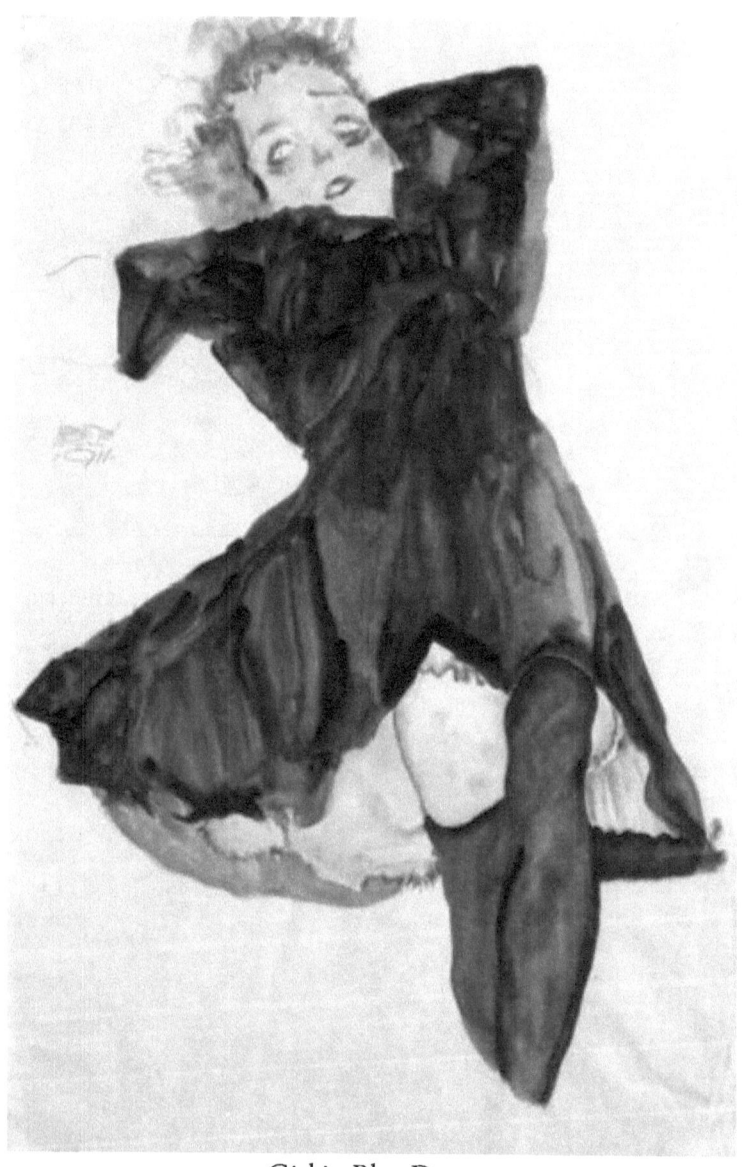

Girl in Blue Dress
1911, watercolor and pencil on paper, 47.8 x 31.7 cm, Private
collection

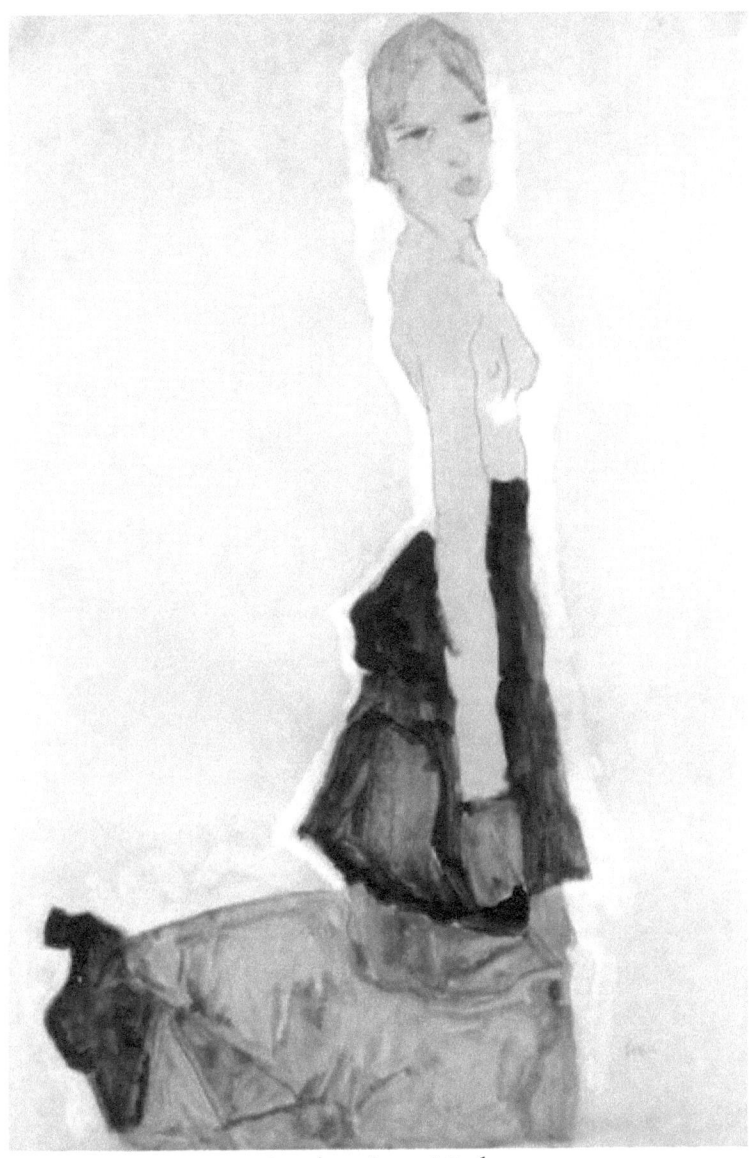

Kneeling Semi-Nude
1911, Gouache, watercolor, pencil and white heightening on
paper, Private collection

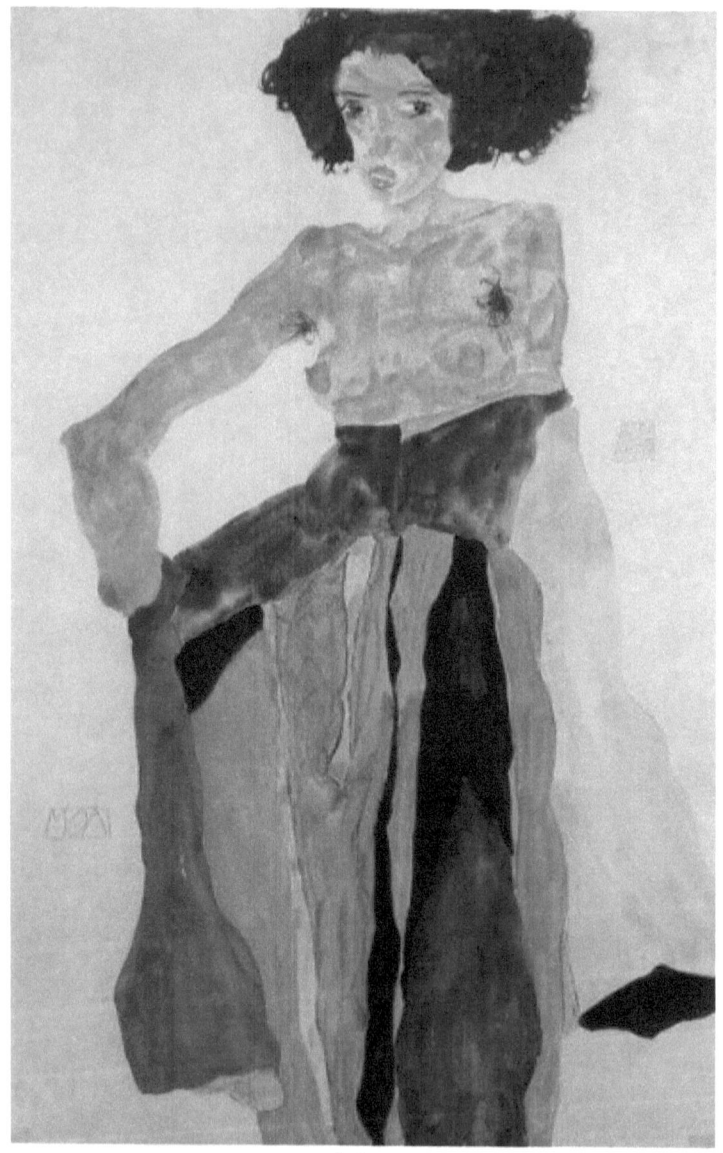

Moa
1911, Gouache, watercolor and pencil on paper, Private
collection

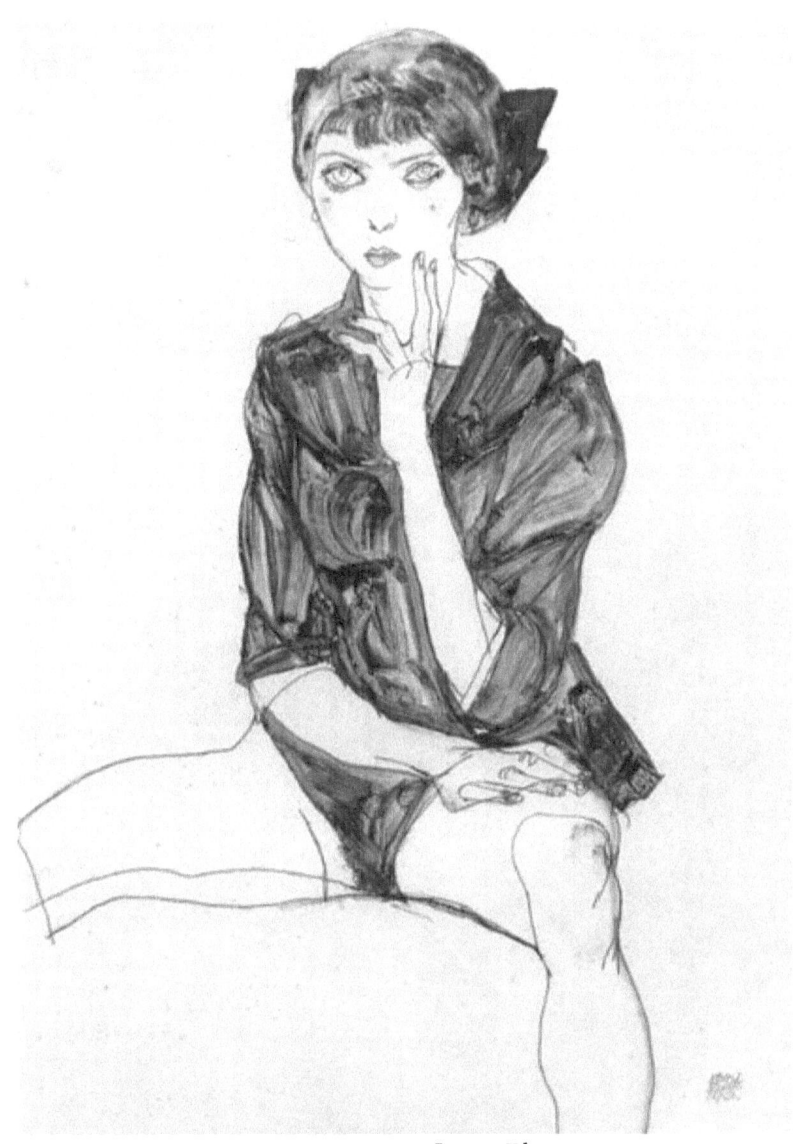

Sitting Woman in a Green Blouse
1913, Gouache, watercolor and pencil on paper, Private
collection

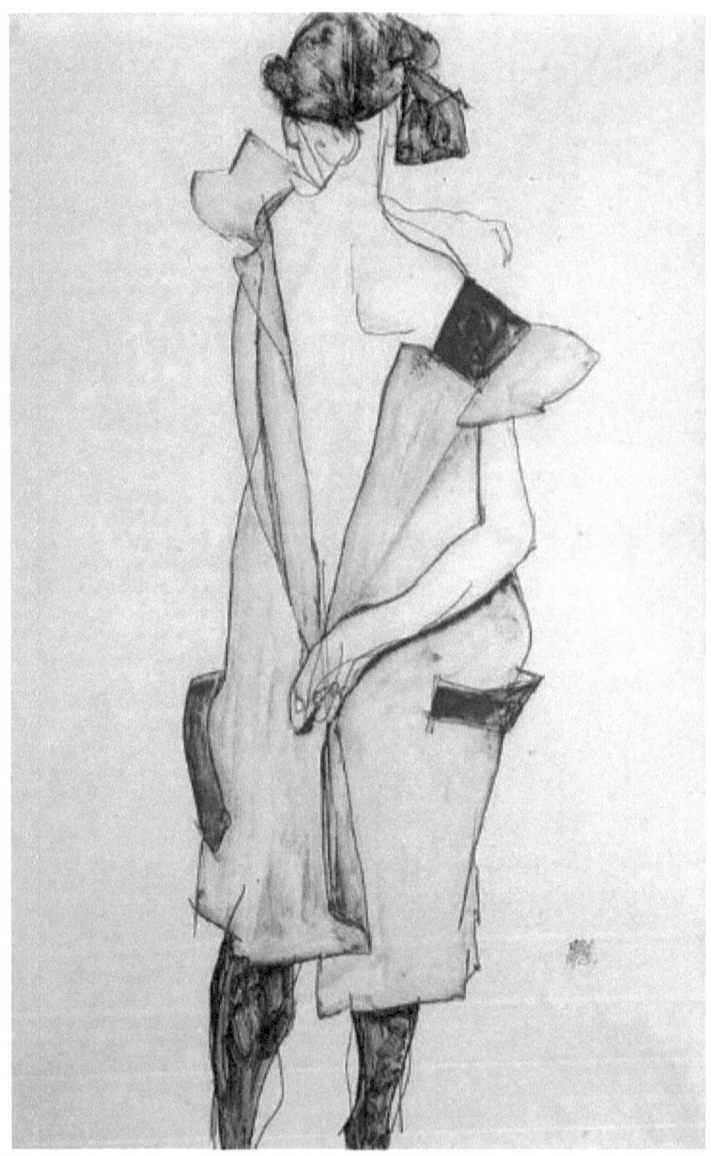

Standing Girl in a Blue Dress and Green Stockings, Back View
1913, Watercolor and pencil on paper, Private collection

EGON SCHIELE

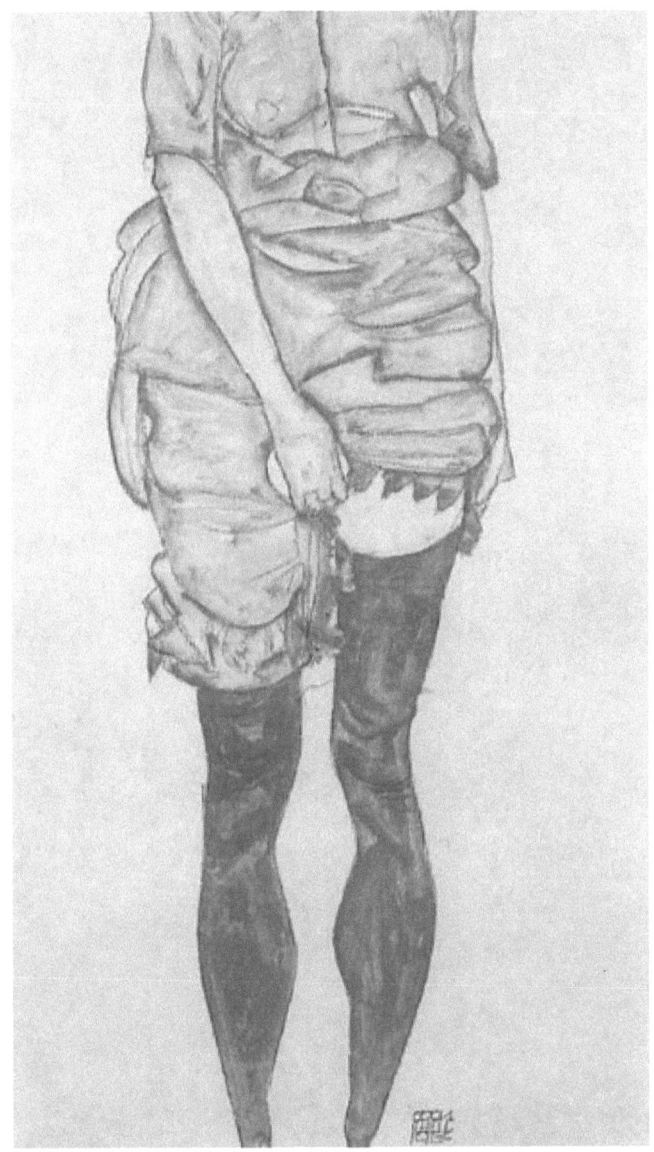

Standing Woman in Red
1913, Gouache, watercolor and pencil, Private collection

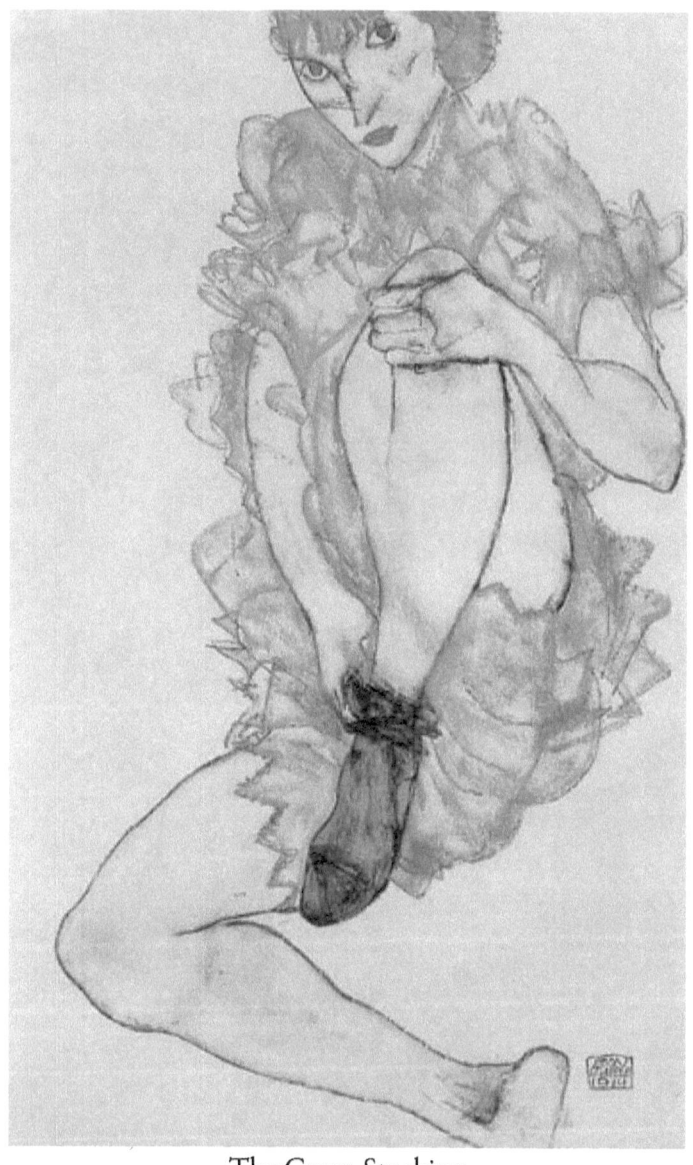

The Green Stocking
1914, Gouache and pencil on paper, Private collection

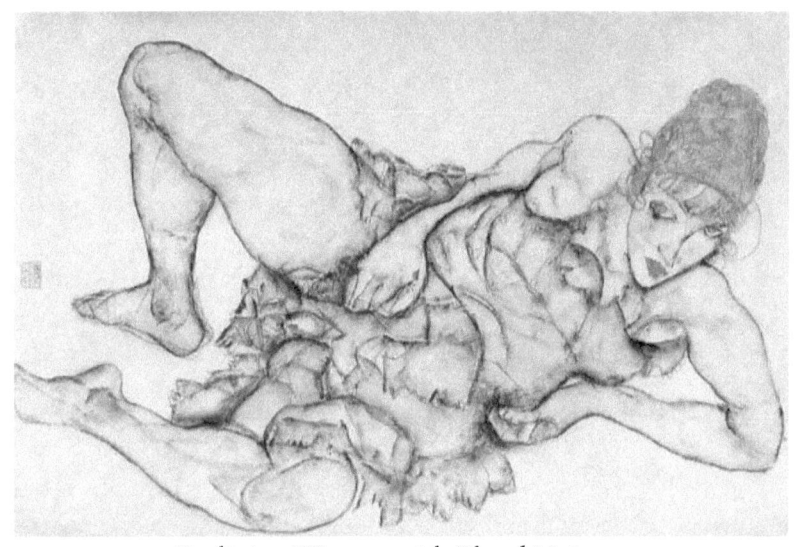

Reclining Woman with Blond Hair
1914, Gouache, watercolor and pencil on paper, Baltimore
Museum of Art

Jessica Findley

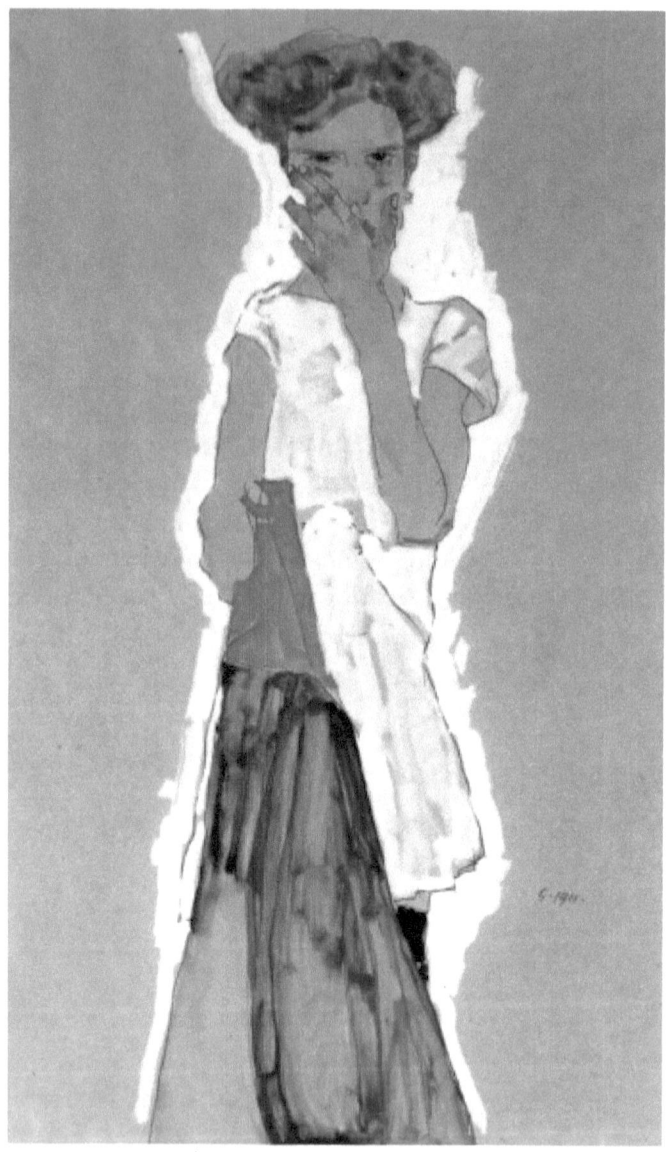

Standing Girl in White Underwear
1911, Gouache, watercolor and pencil on paper, Private
collection

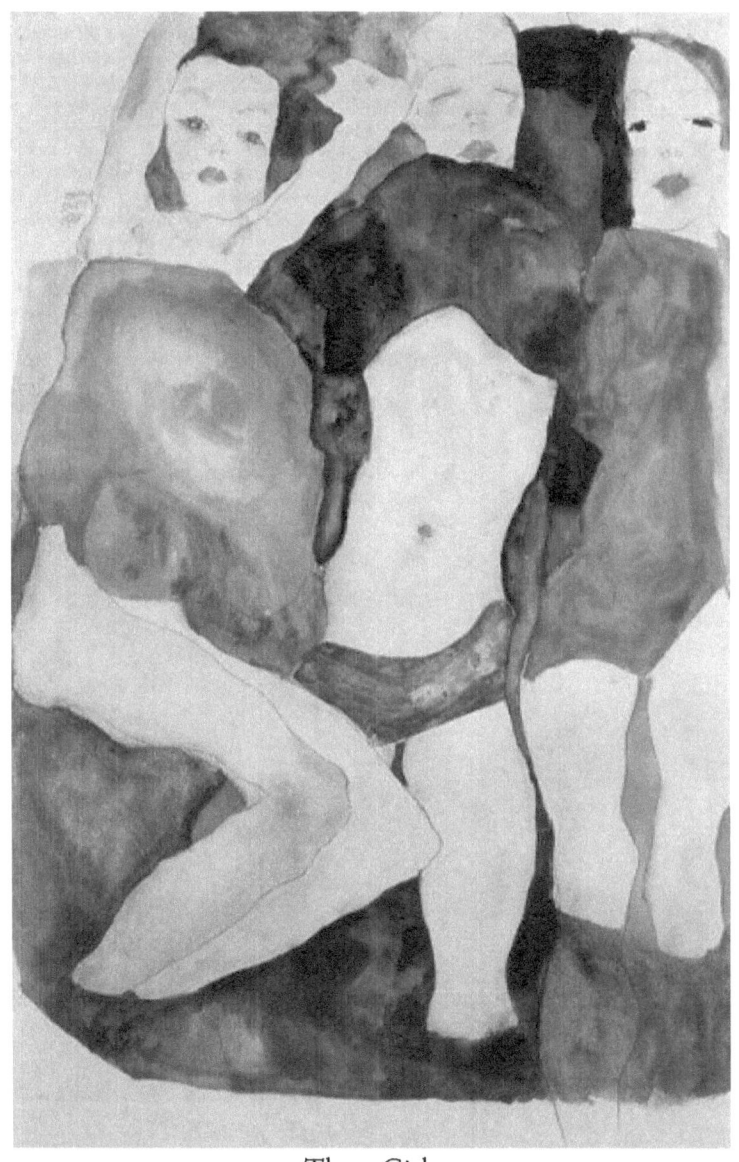

Three Girls
1911, watercolor, Private collection

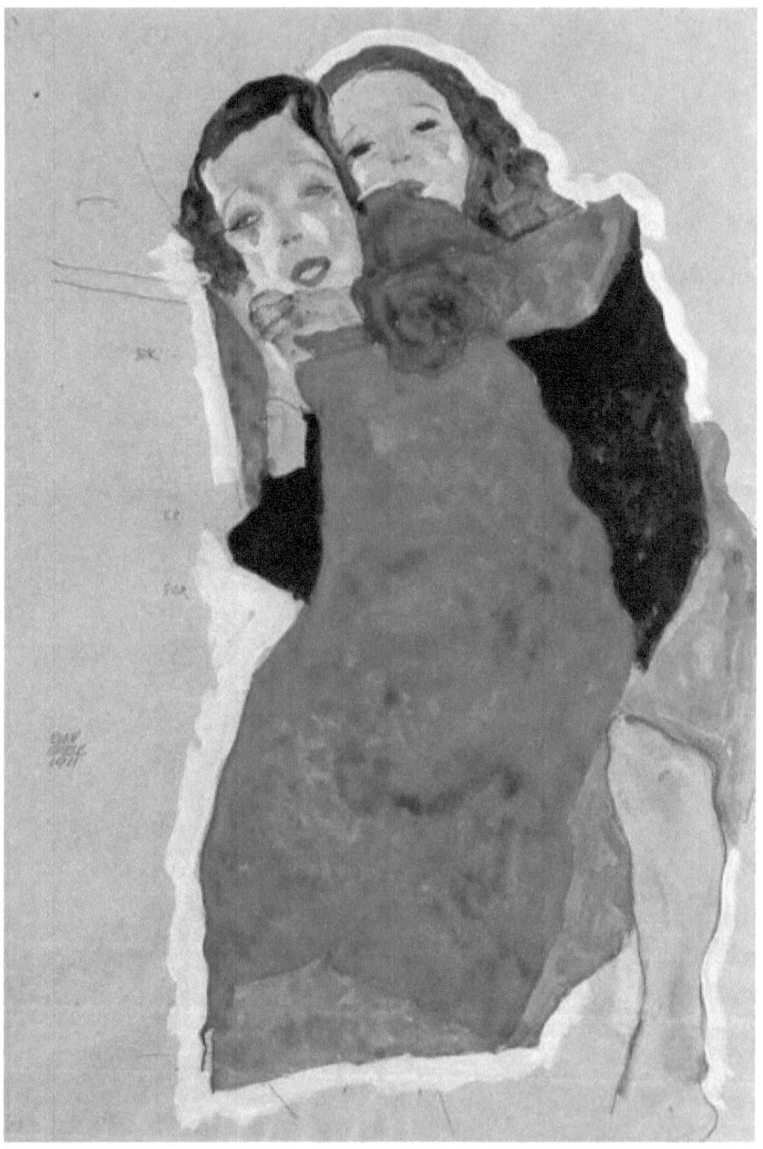

Two Girls
1911, Pencil, watercolor, gouache and white body color, Private collection

EGON SCHIELE

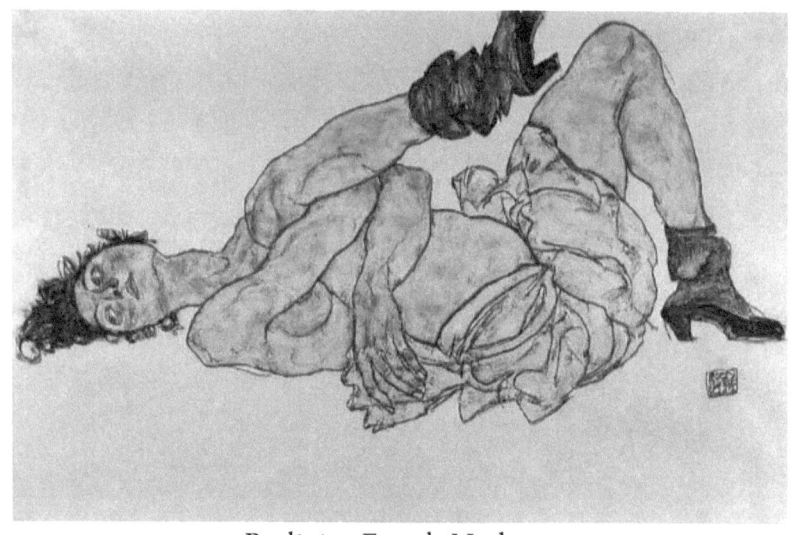

Reclining Female Nude
1917, Gouache, watercolor and charcoal, Private collection

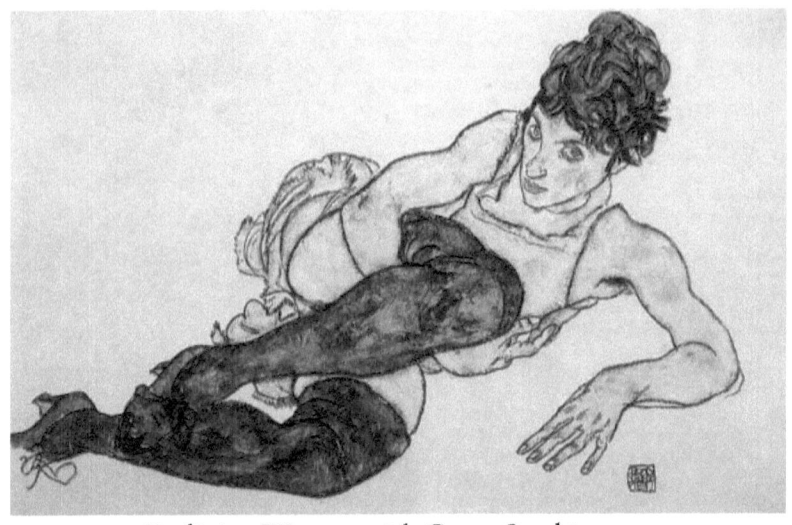

Reclining Woman with Green Stockings
1917, Gouache and black crayon on paper, Private collection

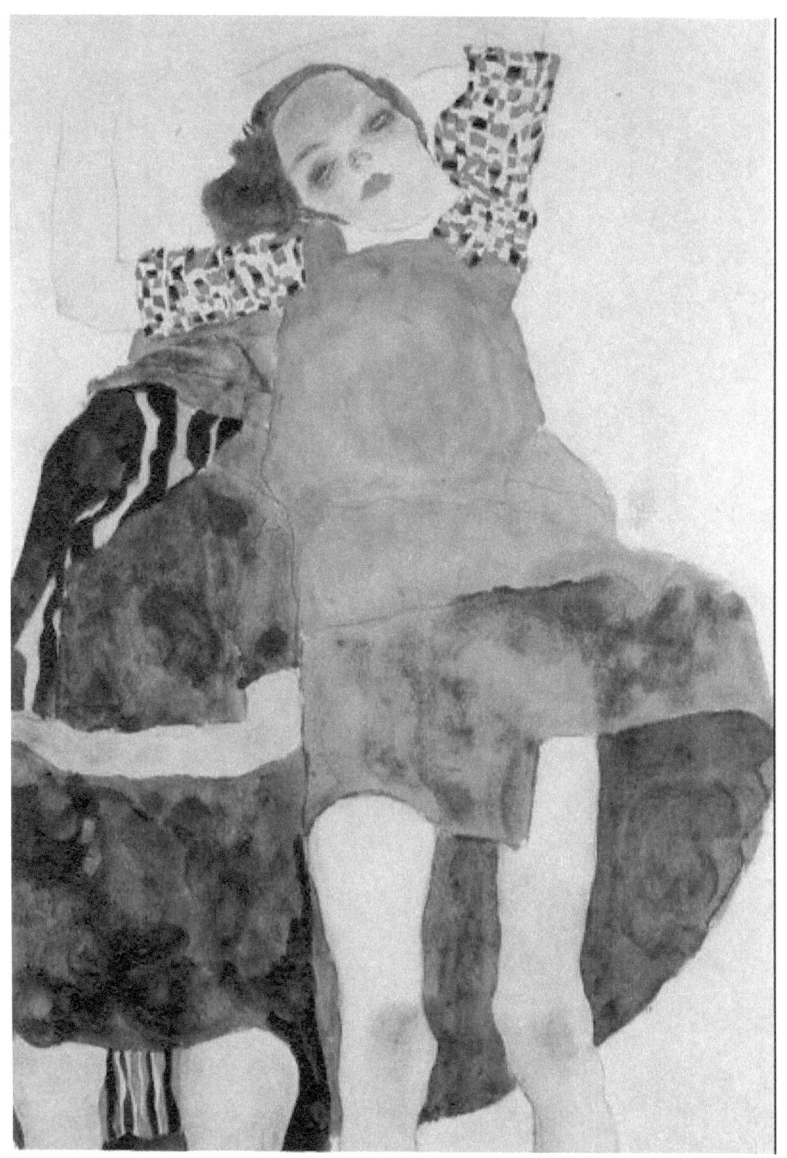

Two Seated Girls
1911, watercolor, Private collection

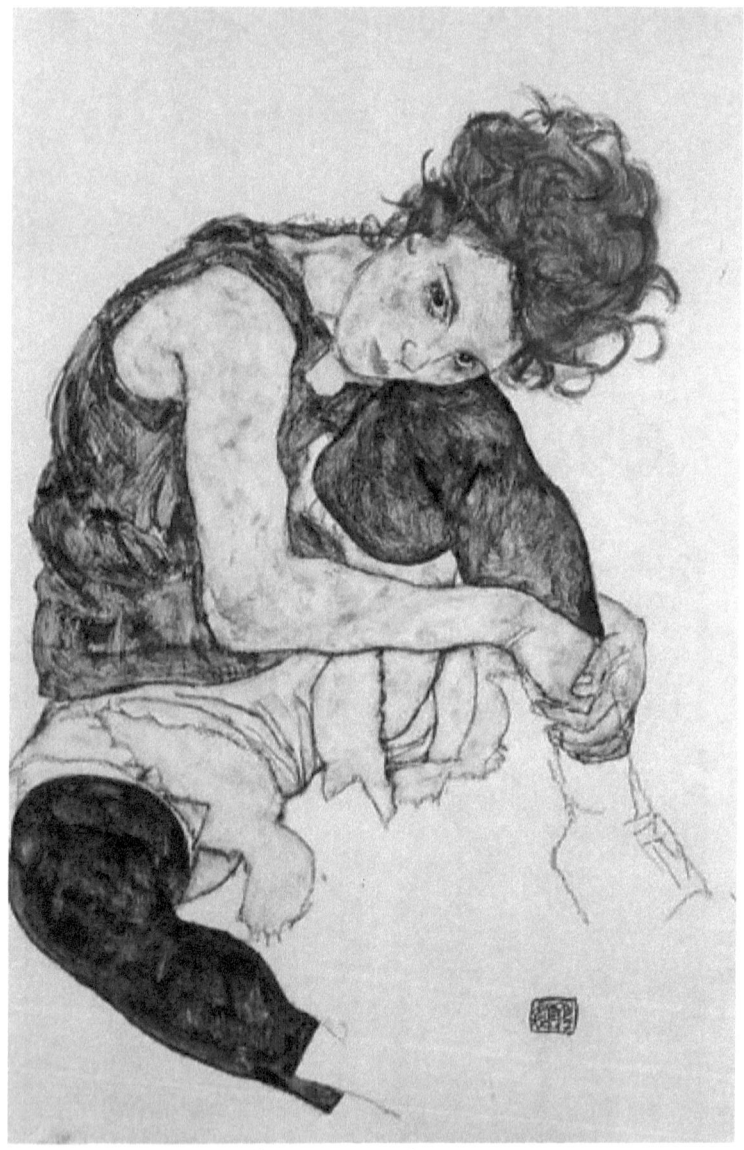

Seated Woman with Bent Knee
1917, Gouache, watercolor and pencil on paper, National
Gallery - Prague

EGON SCHIELE

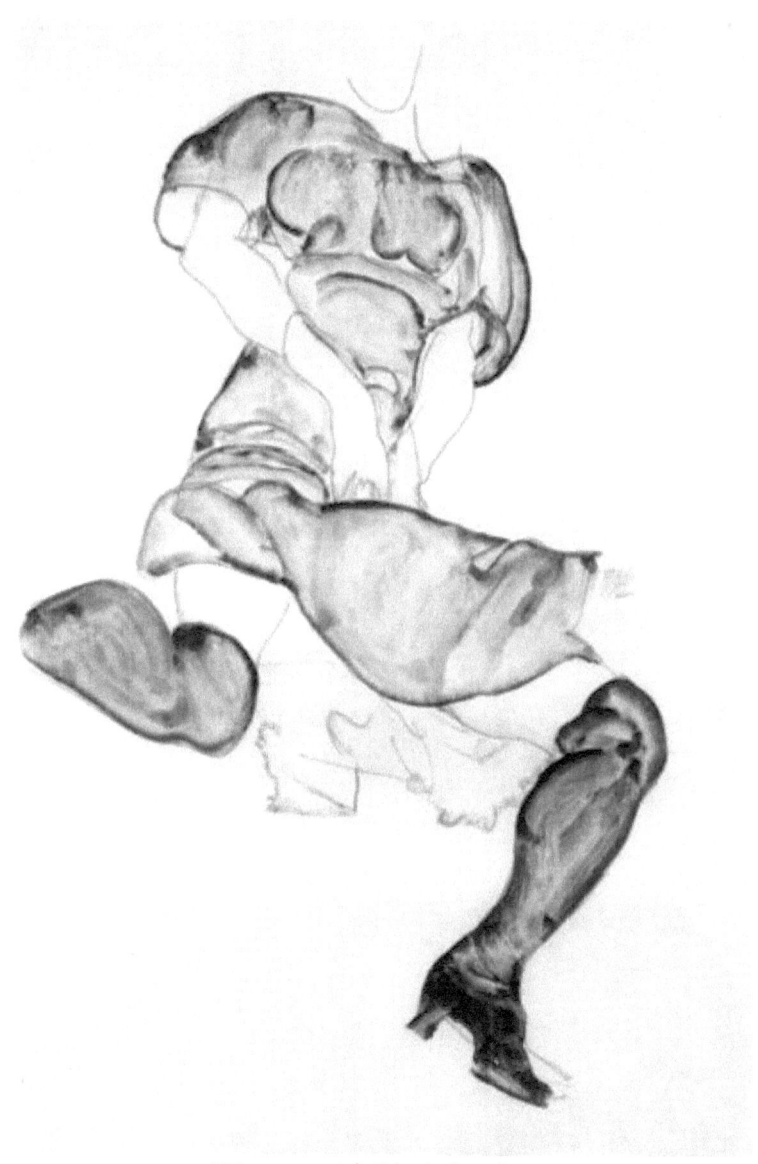

Woman with Black Stockings
1912, watercolor and pencil on paper, Private collection

Jessica Findley

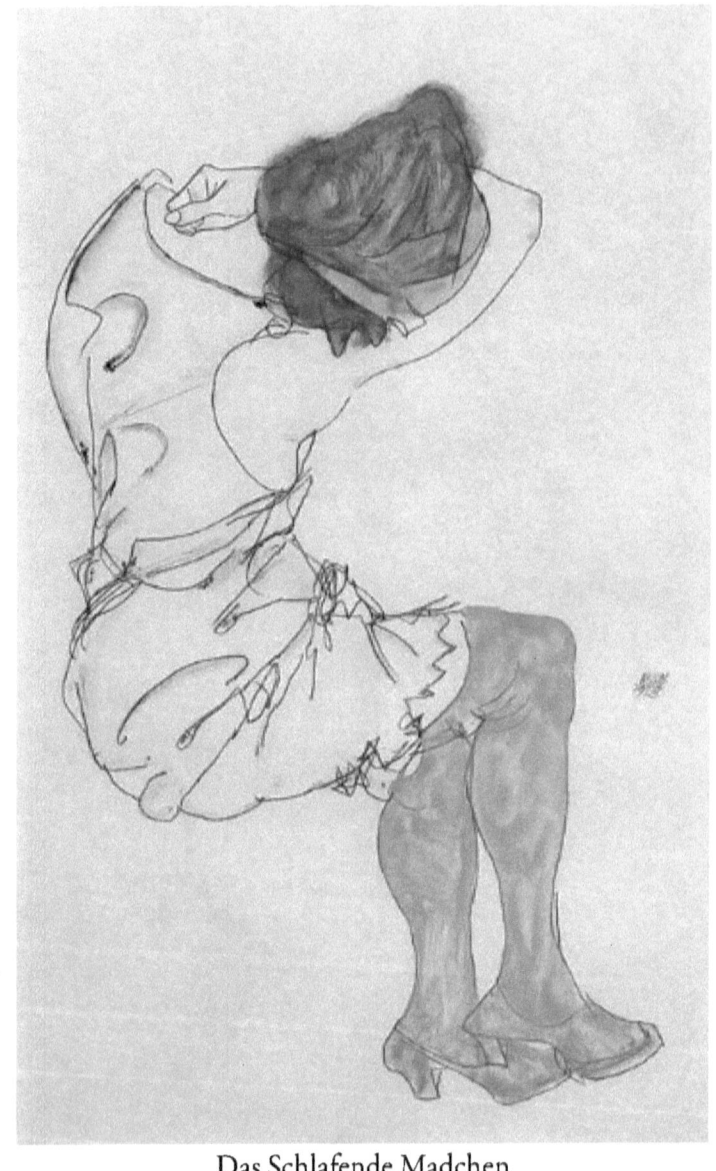

Das Schlafende Madchen
1913, Gouache, watercolor and pencil on paper, Private
collection

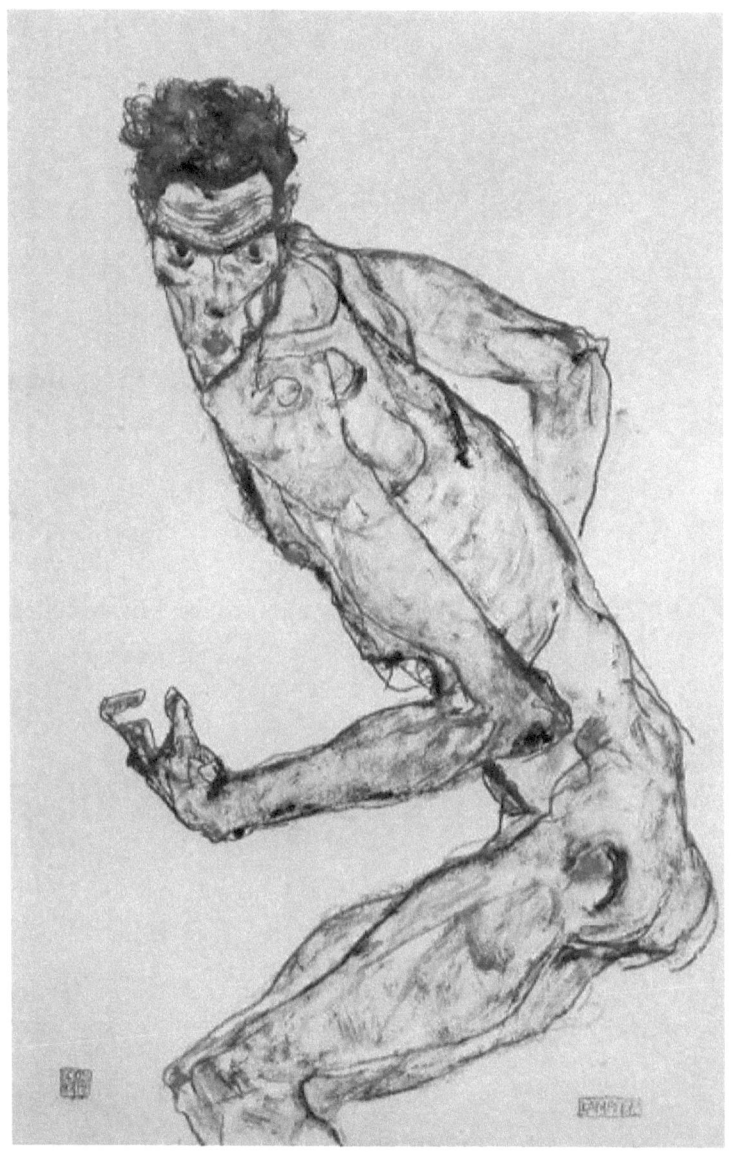

Fighter
1913, Pencil and gouache on paper, Private collection

Jessica Findley

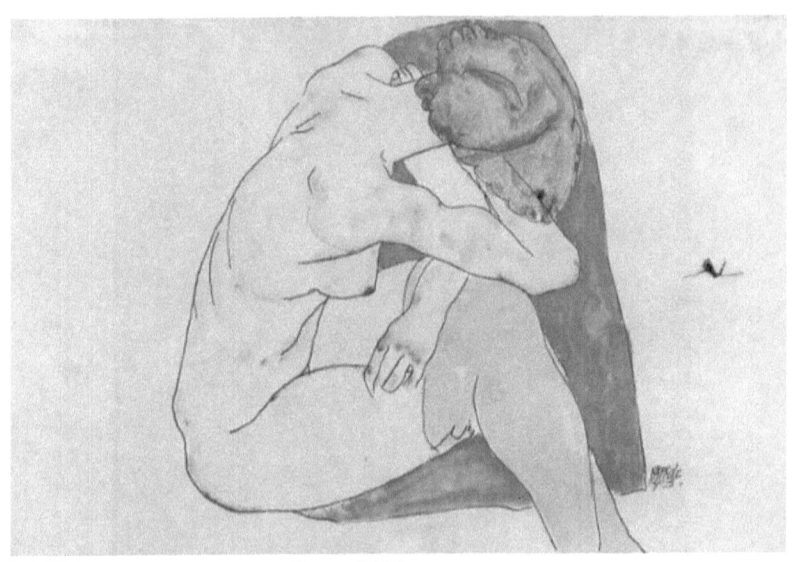

Seated Woman
1913, Watercolor and black crayon on paper, Private collection

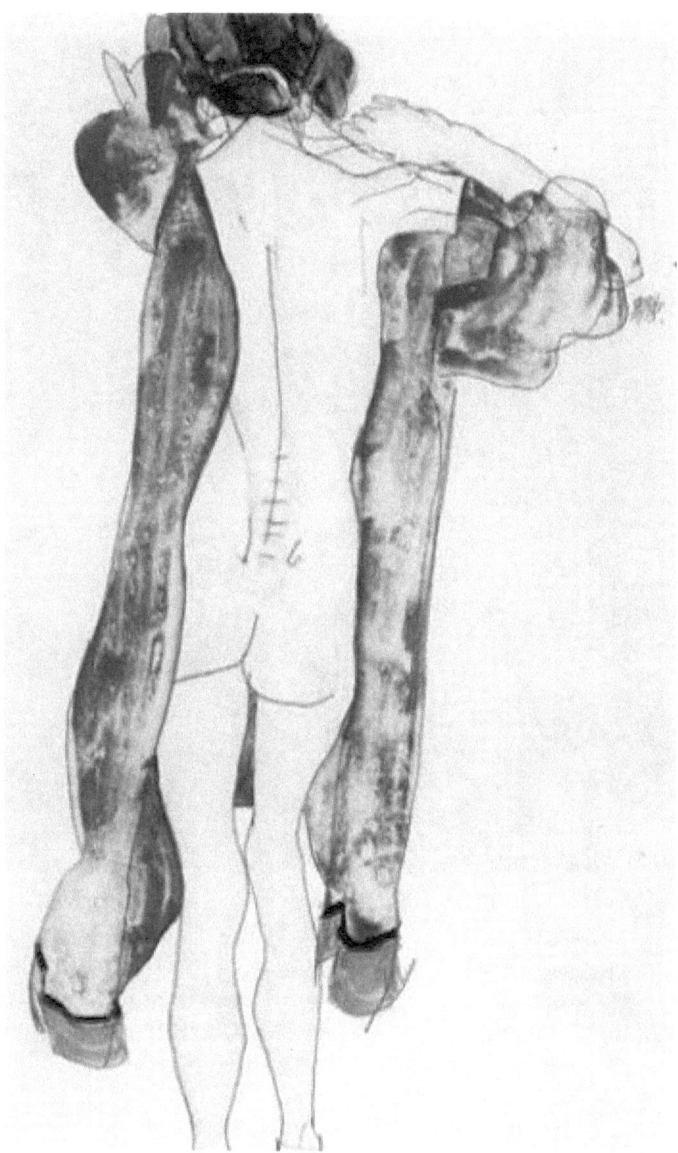

Standing Female Nude in a Blue Robe
1913, Pencil and gouache on paper, Private collection

Jessica Findley

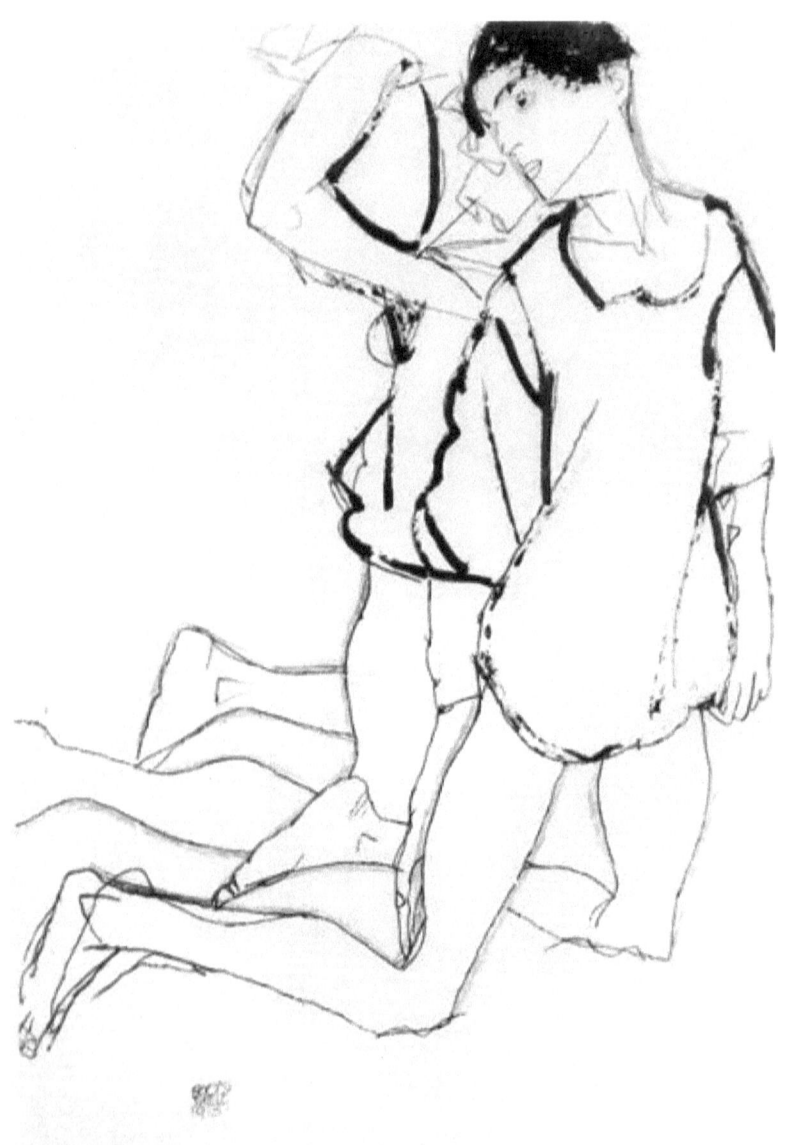

Two Kneeling Figures
1913, Pencil and India ink on paper, Private collection

EGON SCHIELE

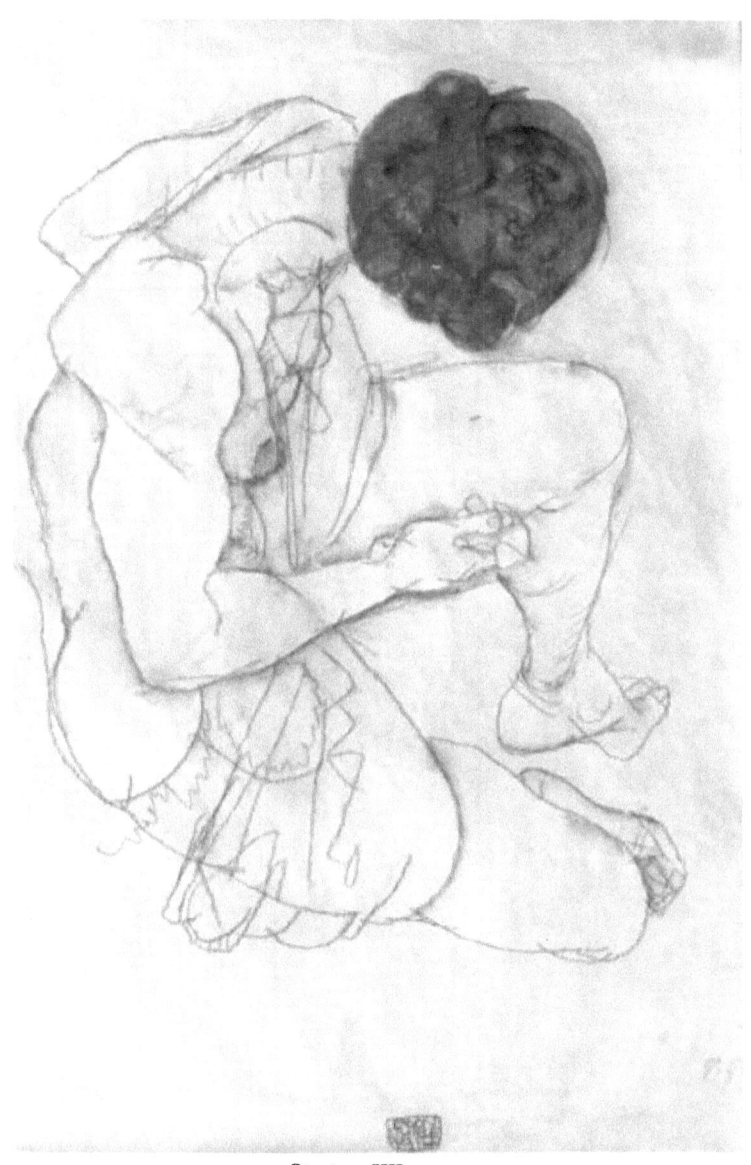

Sitting Woman
1914, Gouache and pencil on paper, Private collection

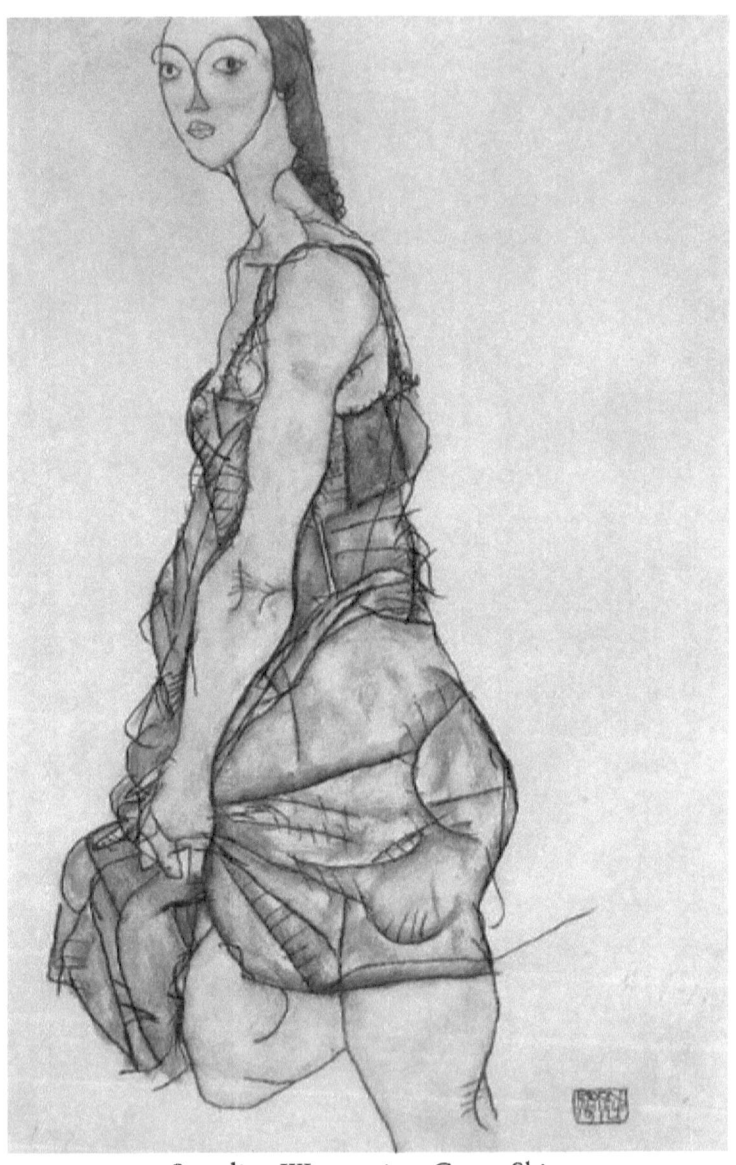

Standing Woman in a Green Skirt
1914, Gouache, watercolor and pencil on paper, Private
collection

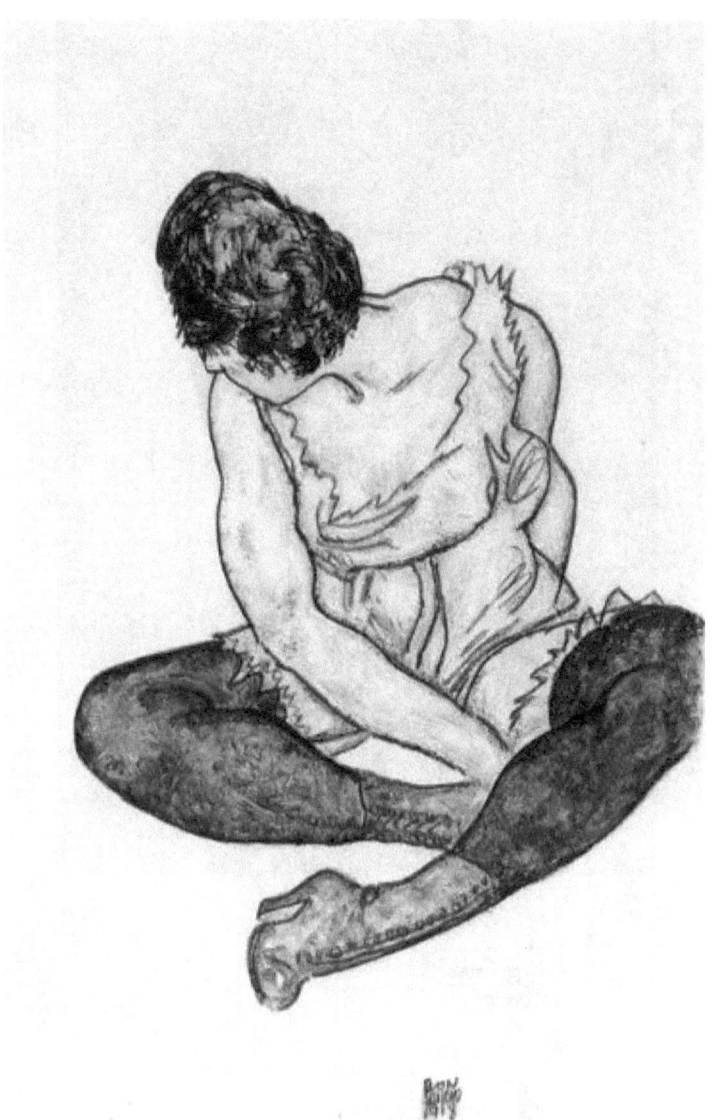

Seated Woman with Green Stockings
1918, Watercolor, gouache and pencil on buff paper, Private
collection

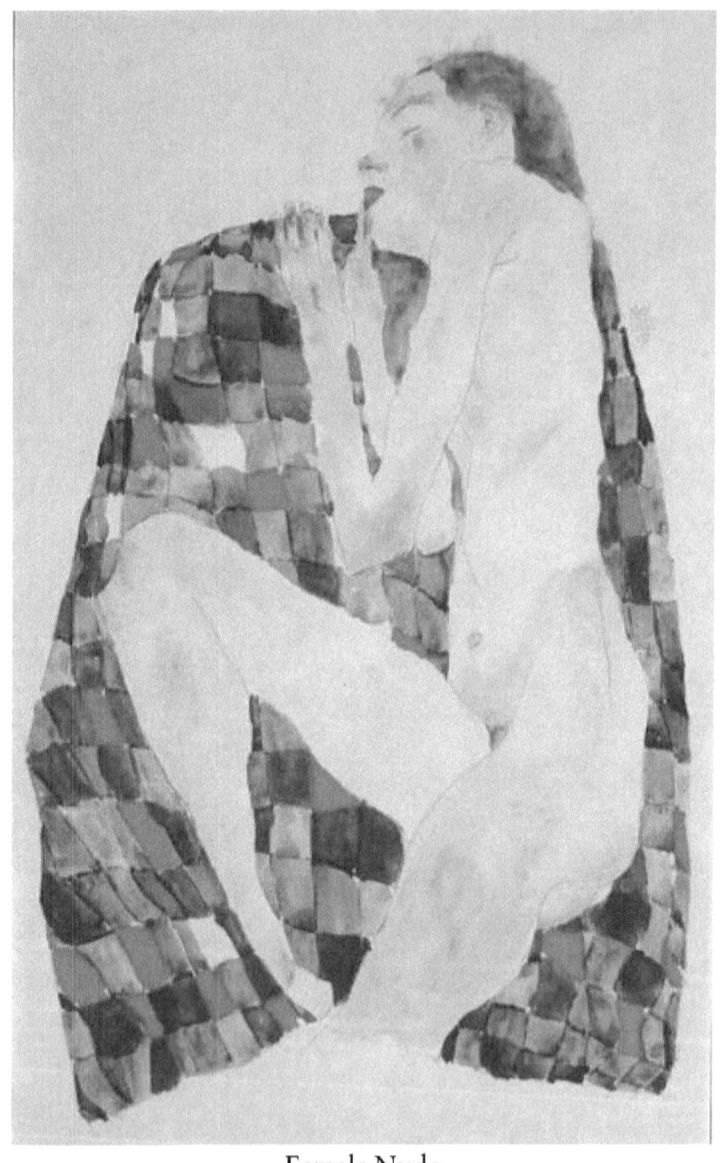

Female Nude
1911, pencil, watercolor, Neue Galerie Graz

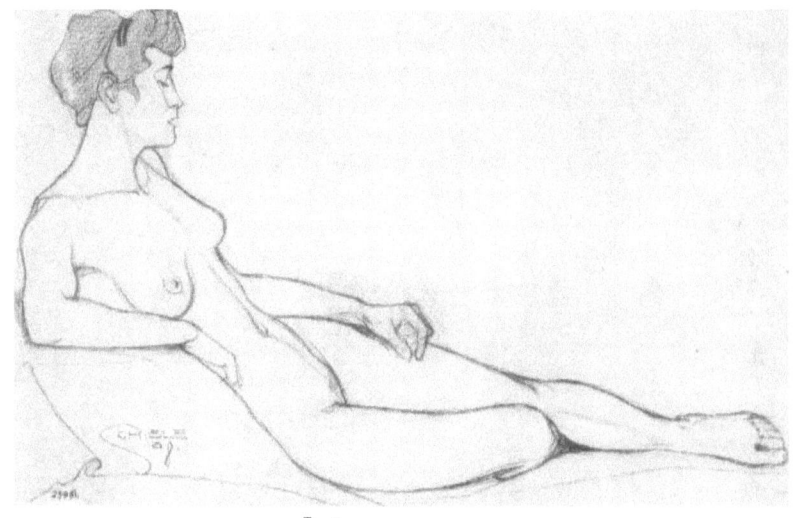

Lying woman
1908, pencil and chalk on paper (blue-gray), Albertina

Jessica Findley

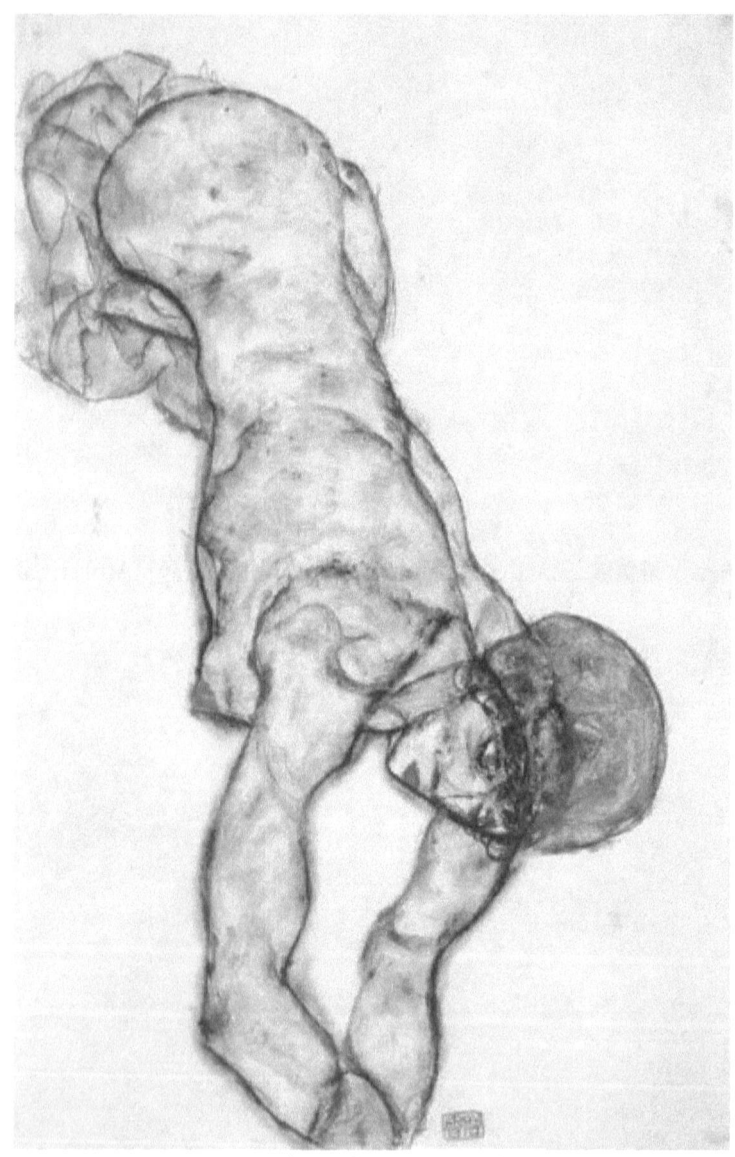

Nude with green hood
1914, watercolor, gouache on paper, Albertina

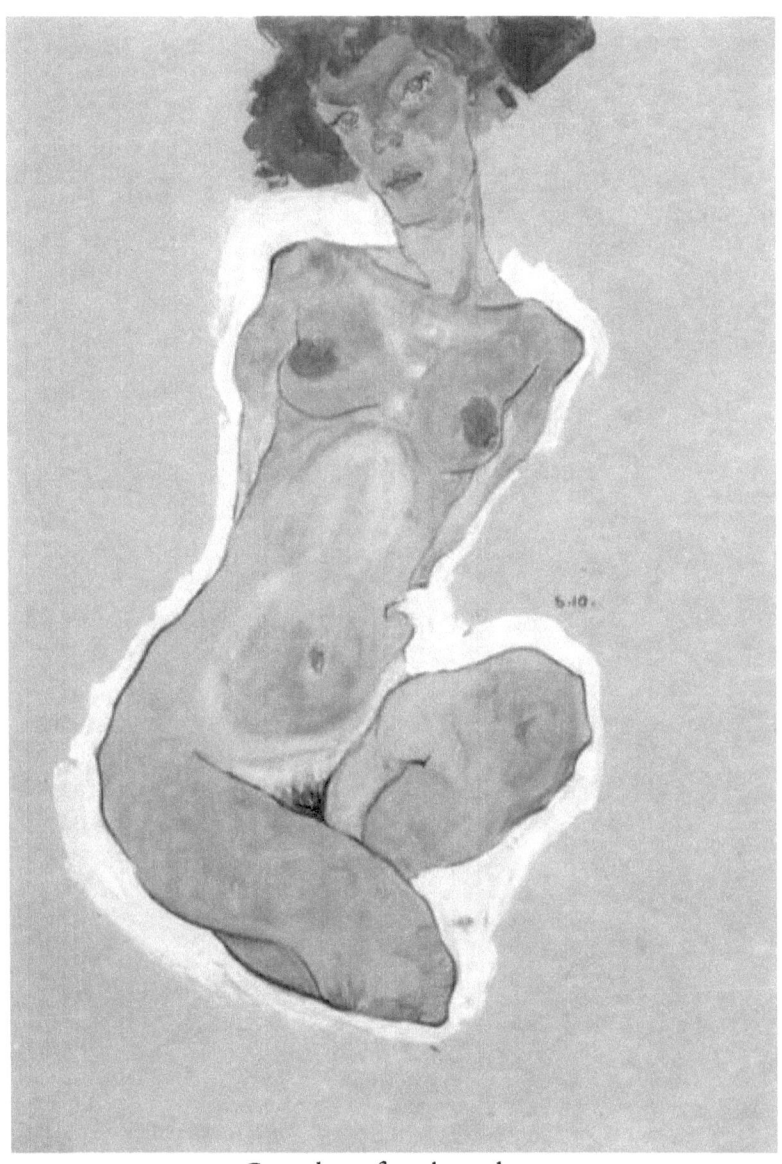

Crouching female nude
1910, chalk, body color on paper, Leopold Collection, Vienna

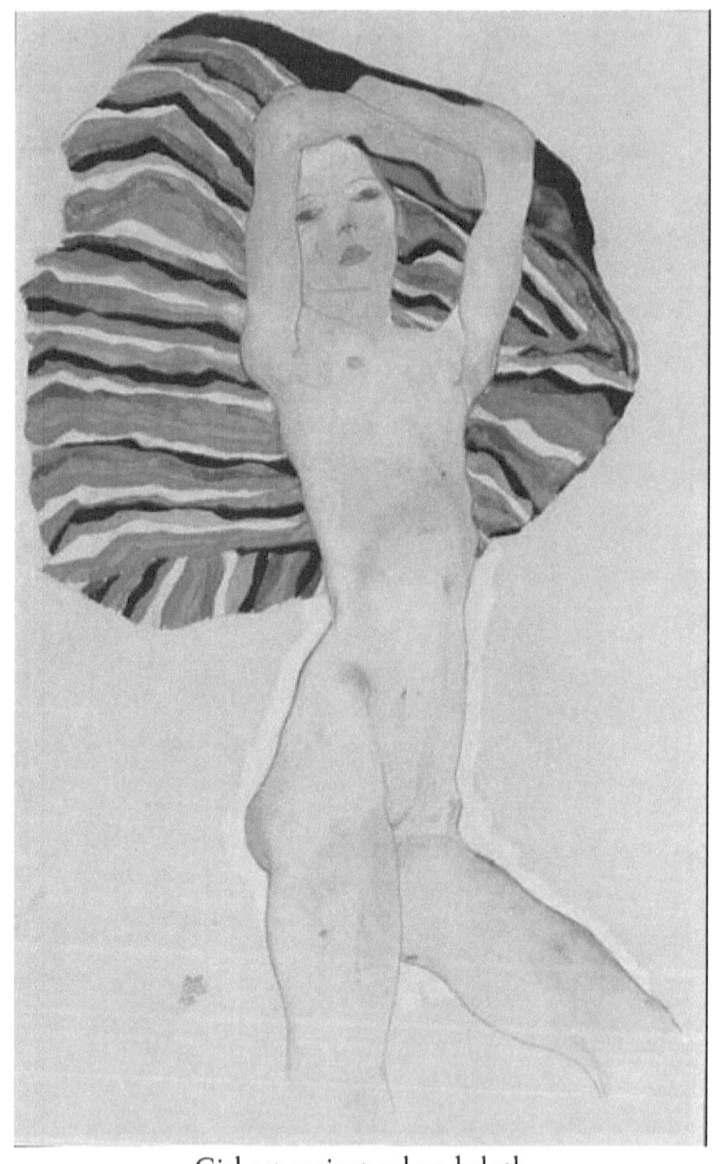

Girl act against colored cloth
1911, Pencil and gouache with watercolor on paper, Public
collection

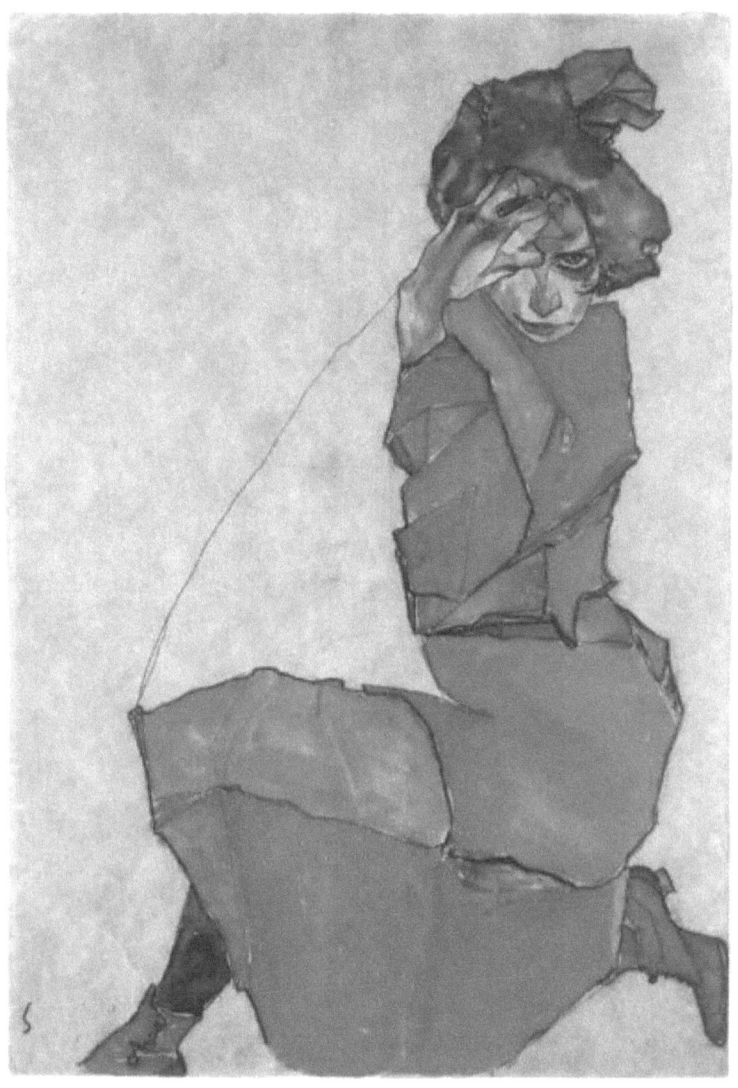

Kneeling girl with red-orange cloth
Date Unknown, Pencil and gouache with watercolor on paper,
Private collection

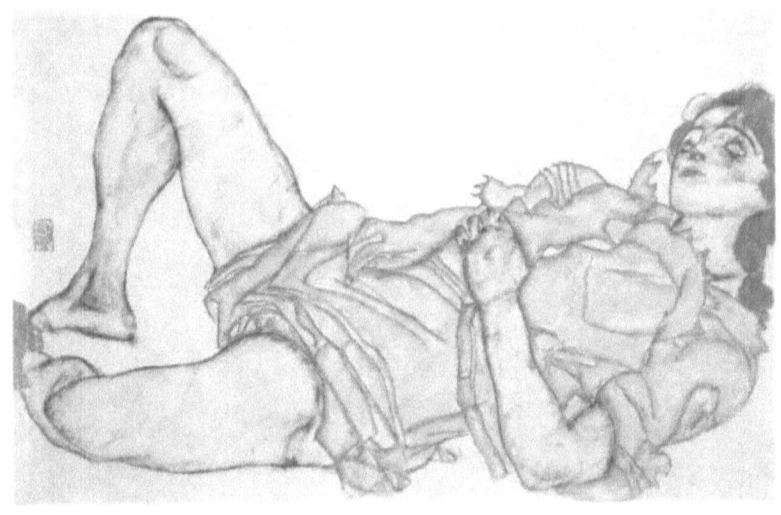

Lying woman with yellow dress
1914, watercolor, gouache on paper, Private collection

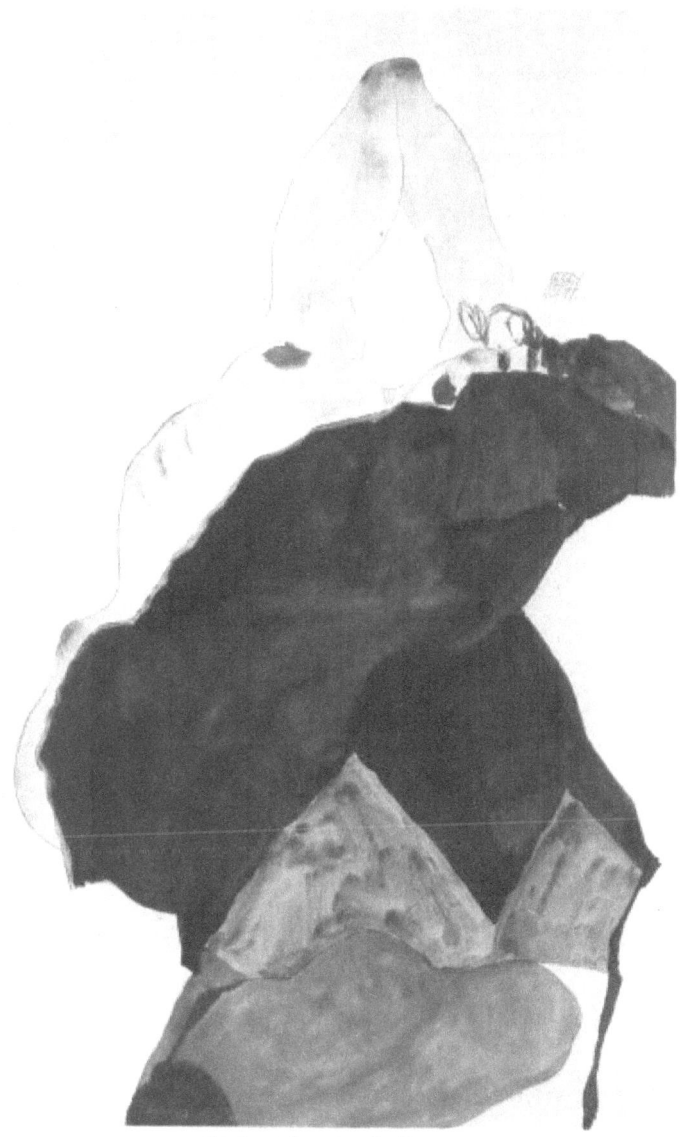

Girl with raised elbow
1911, watercolor, gouache on paper, Private collection

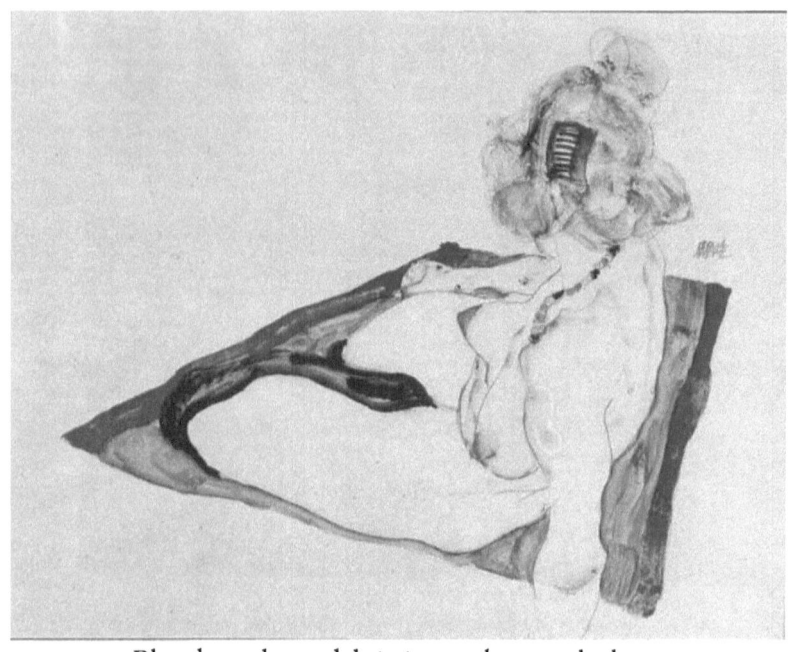

Blonde nude model sitting on brown cloth
1912, watercolor, gouache, pencil on paper, 32 x 48.2 cm,
Albertina, Vienna

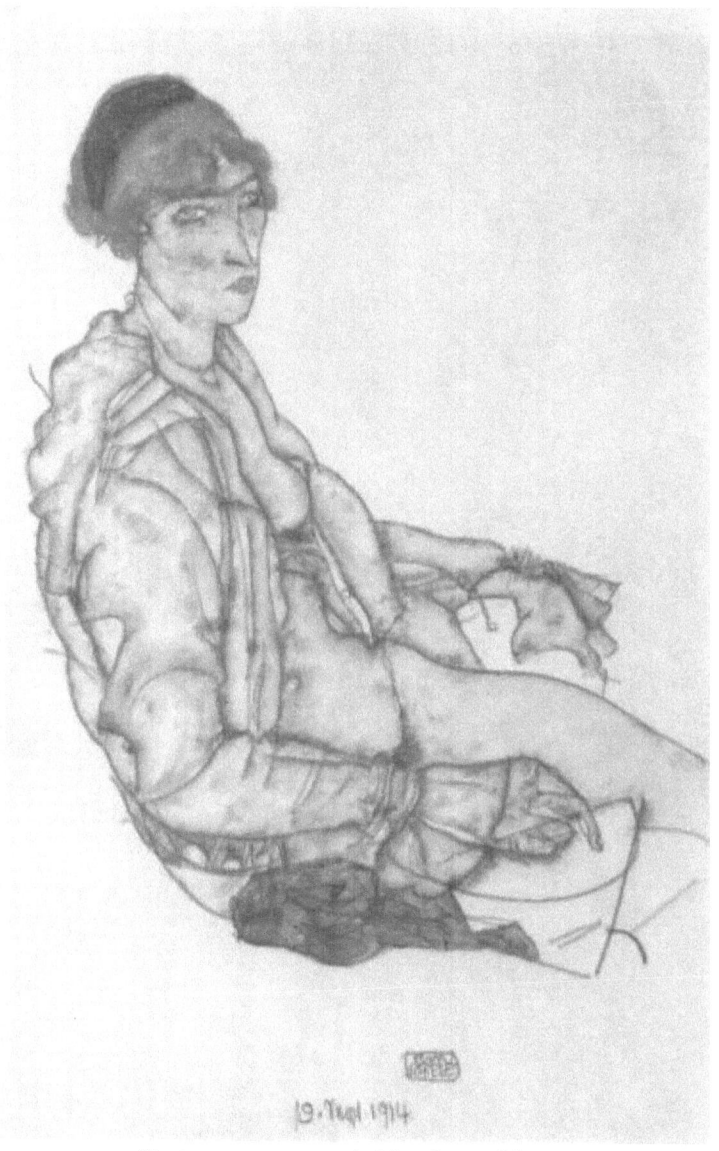

Sitting woman with blue hair ribbon
1914, pencil and watercolor on paper, Leopold Collection

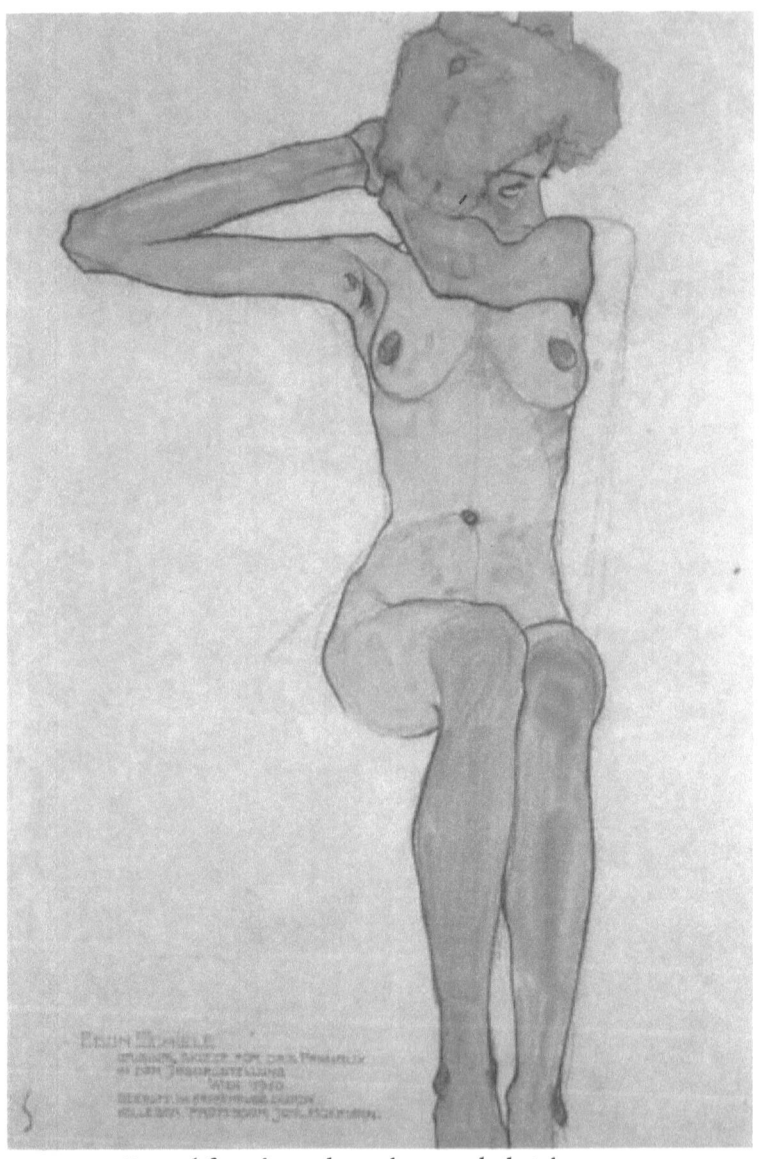

Seated female nude with spreaded right arm
1910, charcoal, watercolor, Public collection

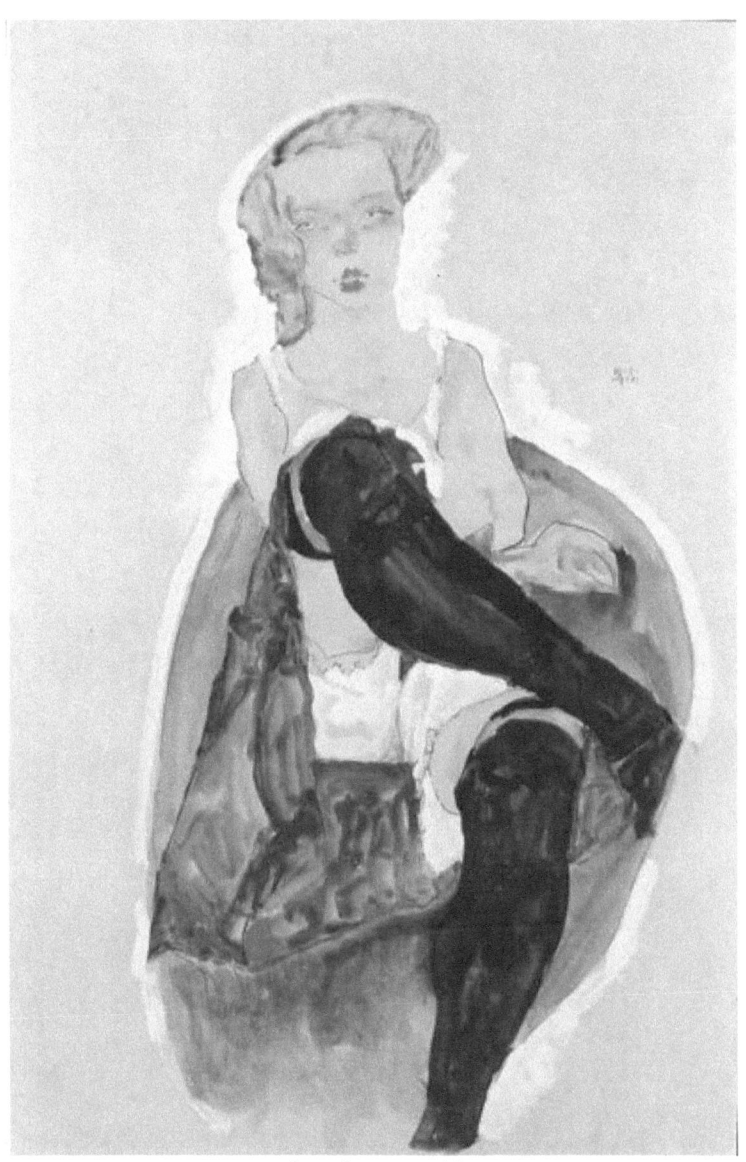

Girl with crossed legs
1911, pencil and gouache on paper, Leopold Museum

Jessica Findley

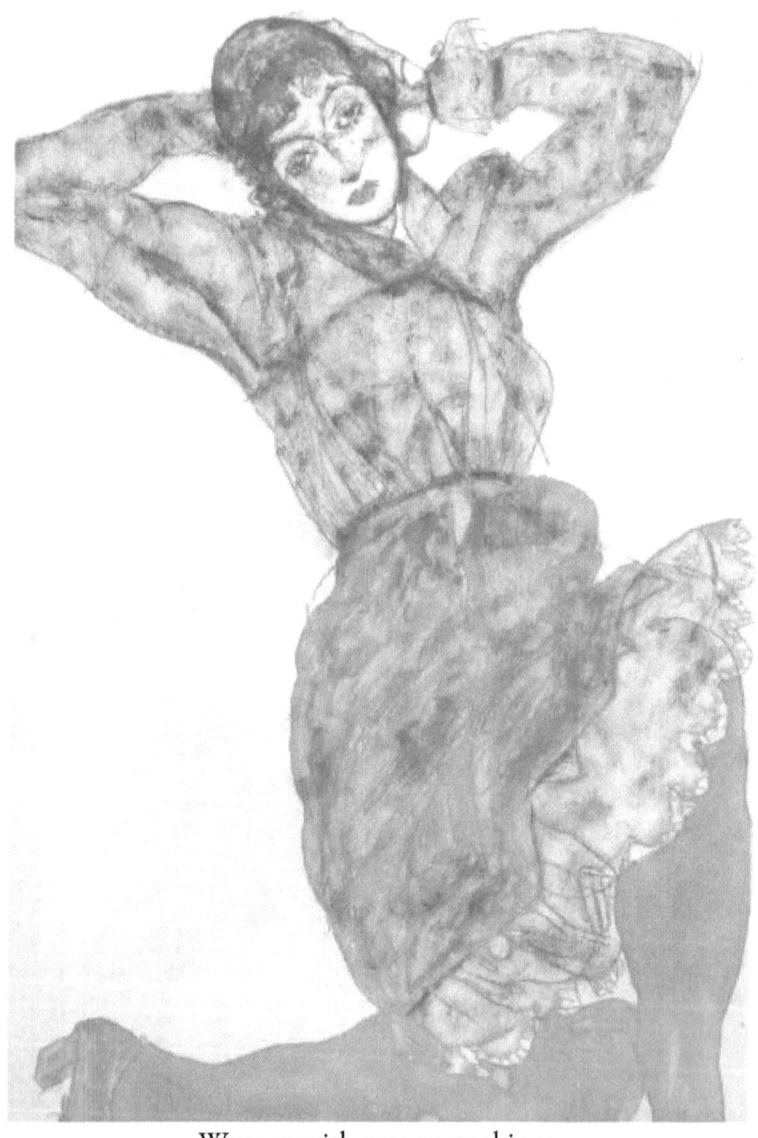

Woman with orange stockings
Unknown date, charcoal, watercolor, Public collection

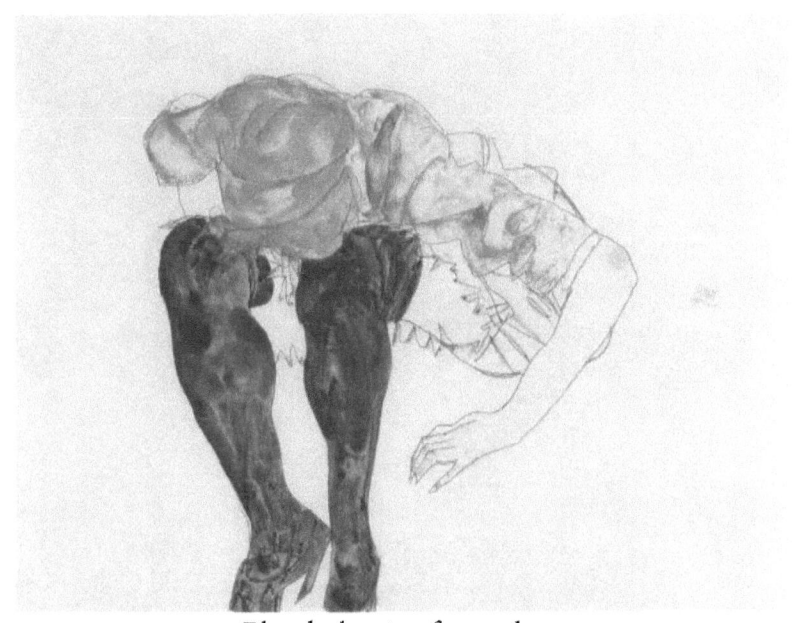

Blonde, leaning forward
1912, pencil, watercolor and gouache on paper, Private
collection

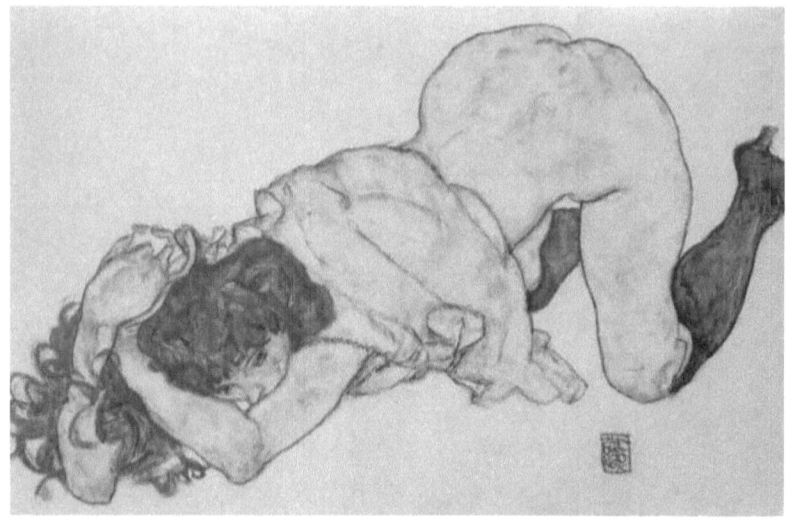

Kneeling girl trimmed on both elbows
1917, chalk on paper, 28.7 x 44.3 cm, Leopold Collection,
Vienna

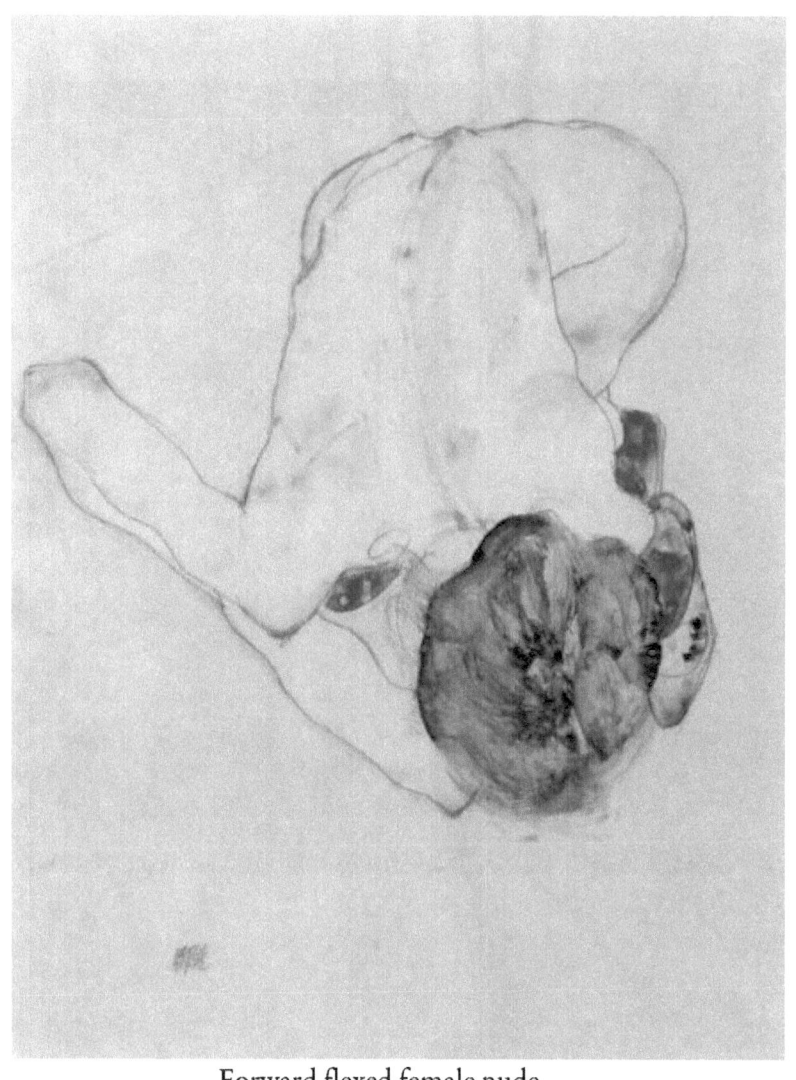

Forward flexed female nude
1912, pencil and watercolor on paper, 37.5 x 28.9 cm, Leopold
Collection, Vienna

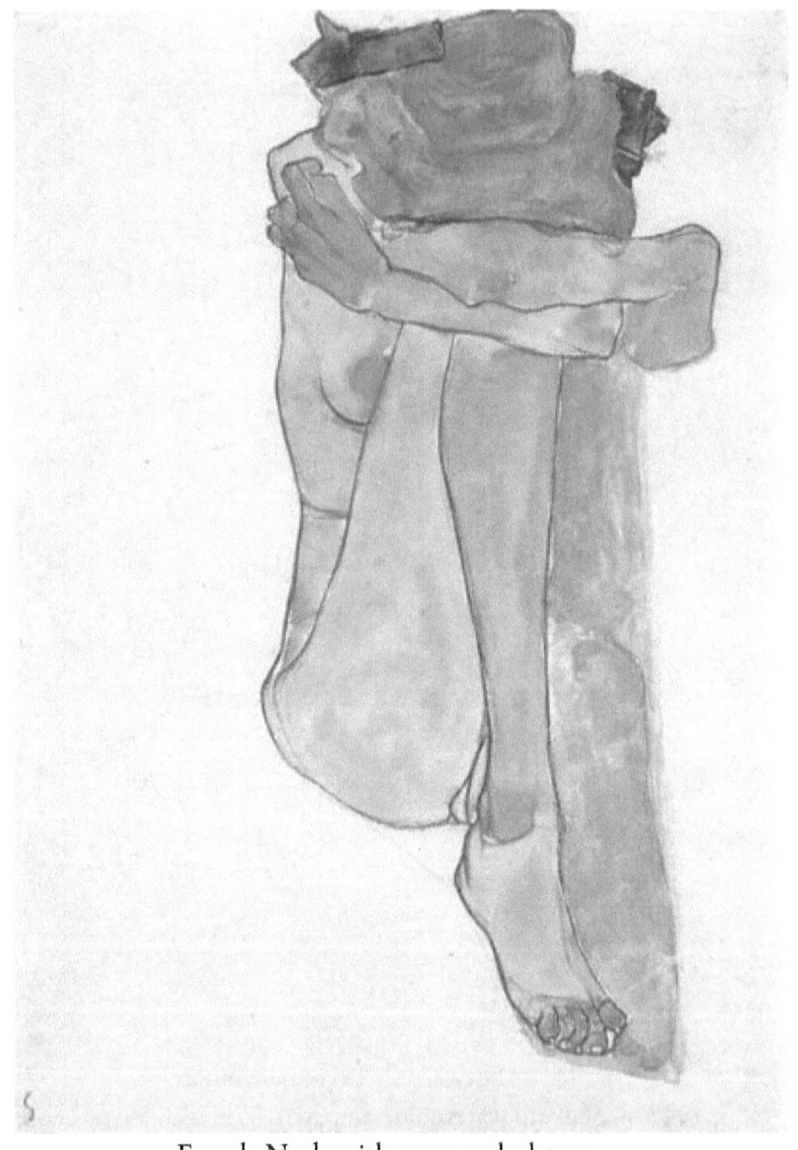

Female Nude with green upholstery
1910, charcoal, watercolor, 44.9 x 32.2 cm, Neue Galerie Graz
am Landesmuseum Joanneum, Graz

EGON SCHIELE

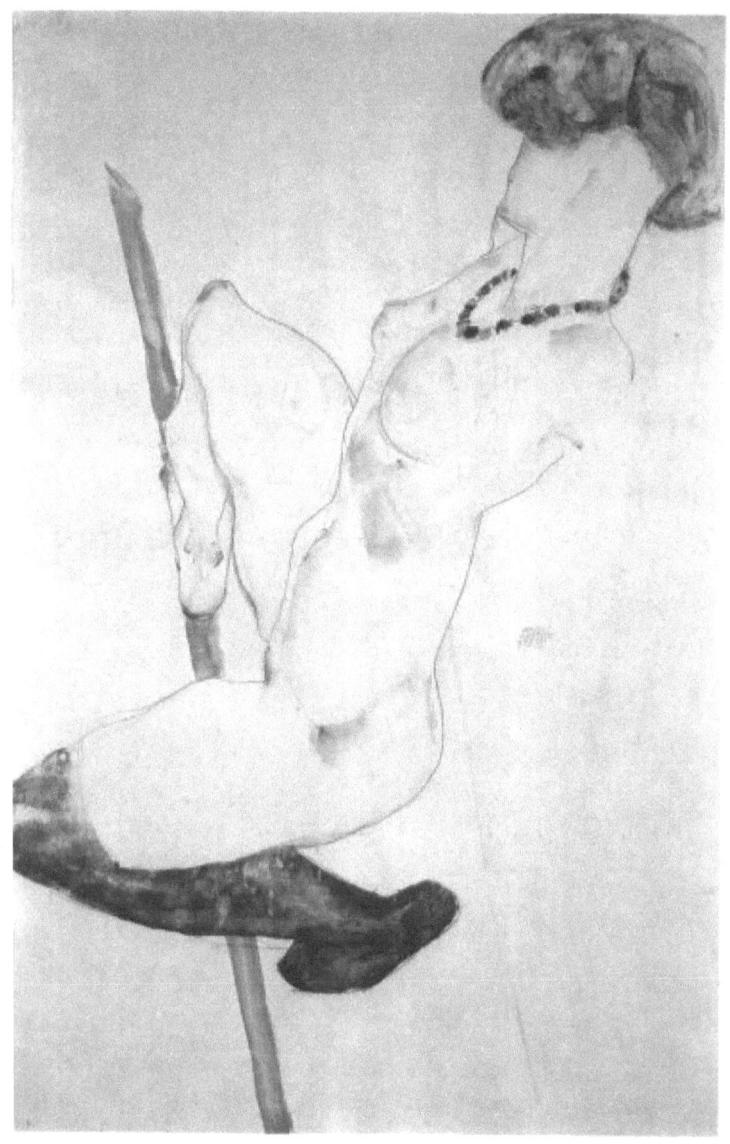

Crouching female nude with bended head
1918, Private collection

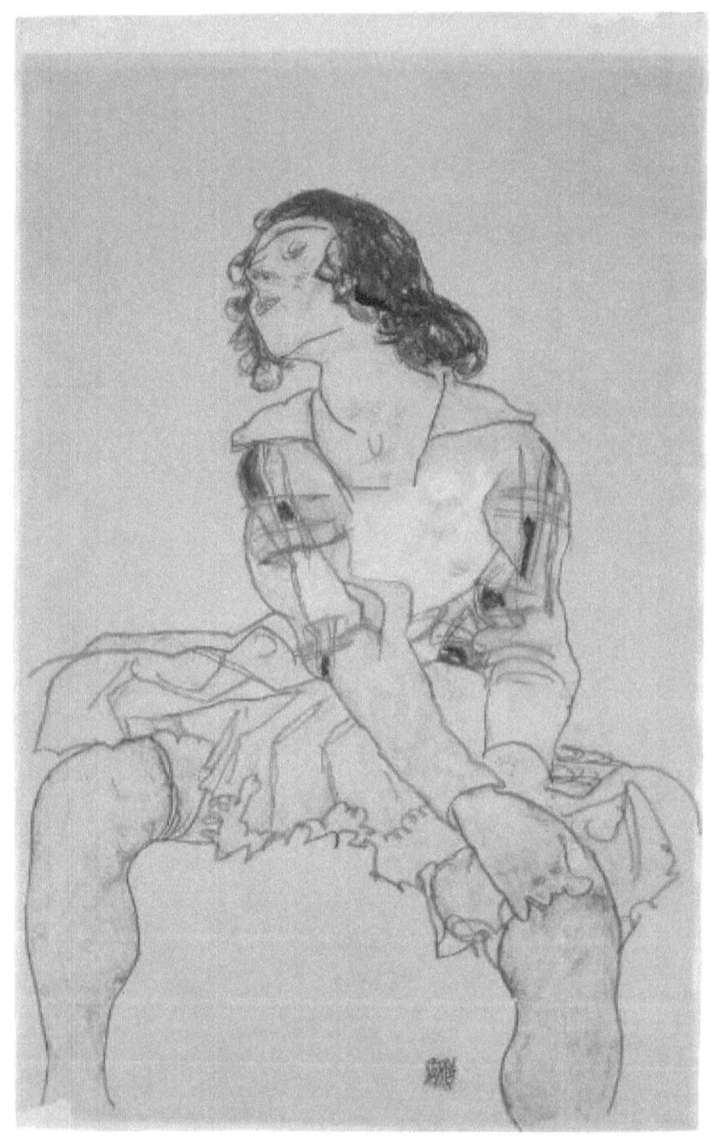

Seating woman
1813, charcoal, watercolor, Private collection

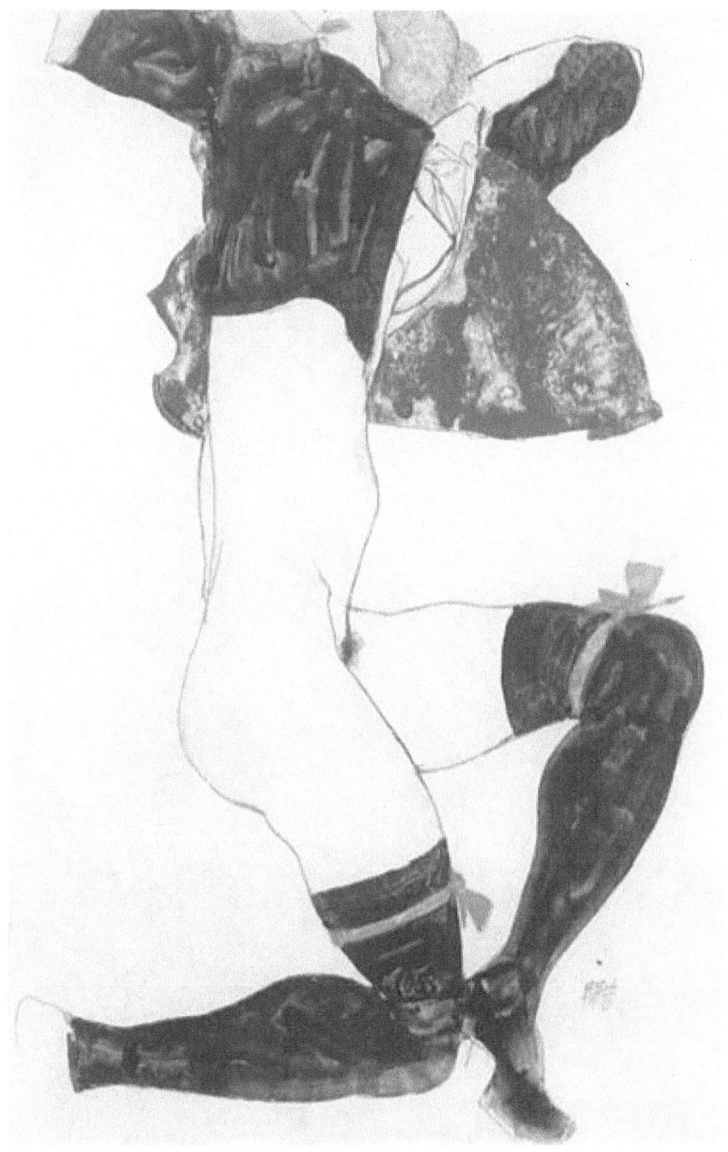

Black Tights
1913, pencil, gouache, 48.3 x 31.4 cm, Private collection

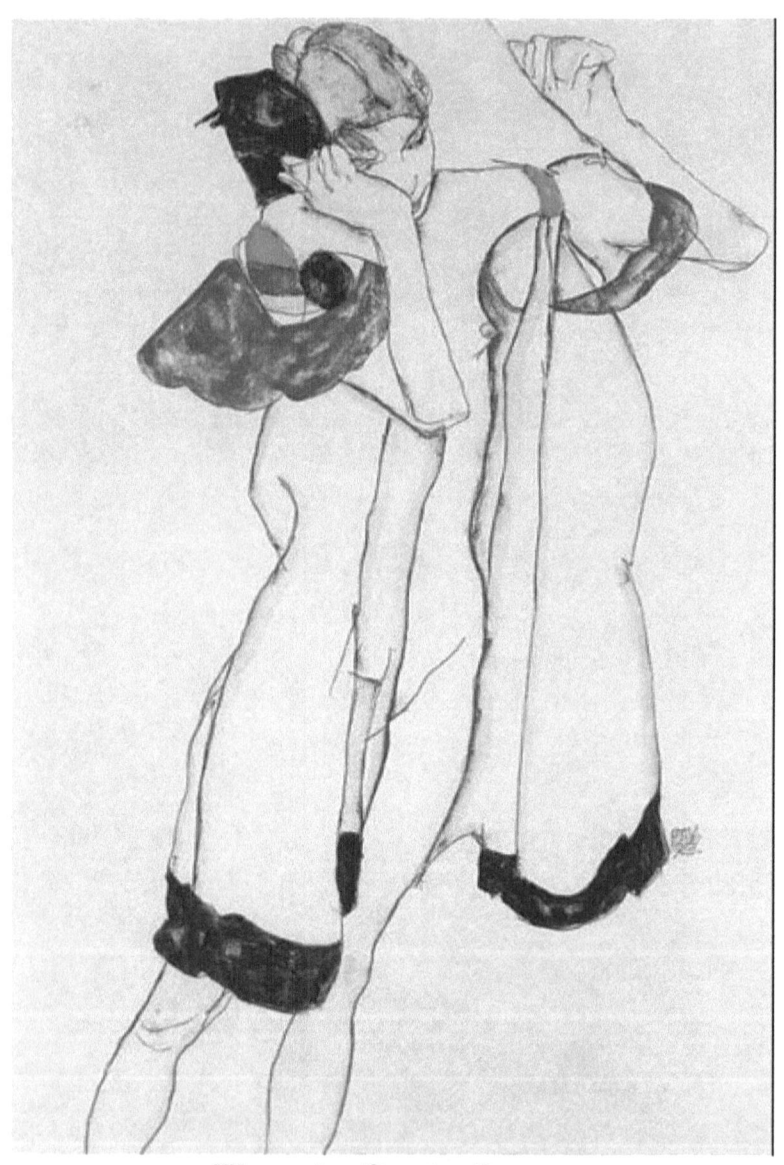

Woman in a Dressing Gown
1913, pencil, watercolor, gouache, 44 x 31 cm, Private
collection

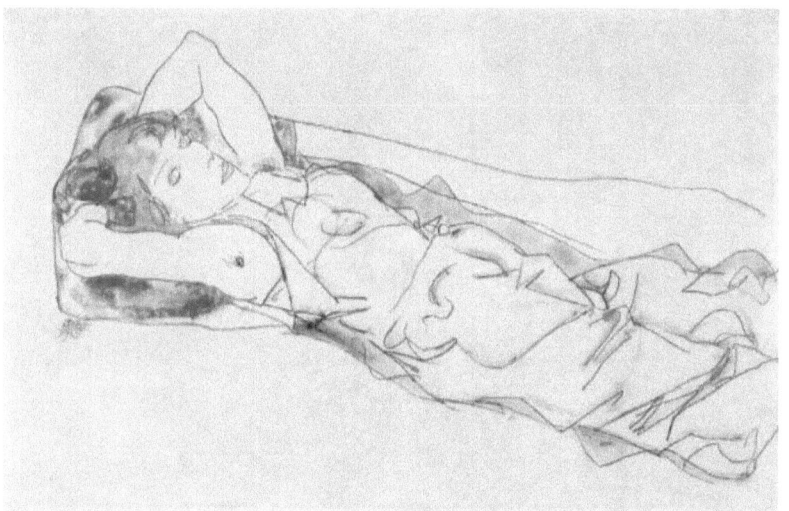

Reclining female figure with gold blonde hair on a blue pillow
1913, pencil, watercolor, gouache, 44 x 31 cm, Private
collection

Jessica Findley

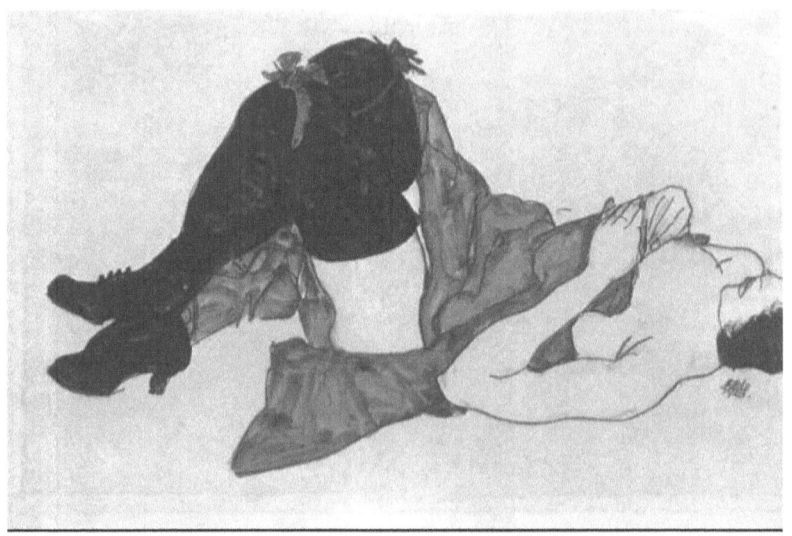

Reclining woman with ochre blanket
1913, pencil, watercolor, gouache, Private collection

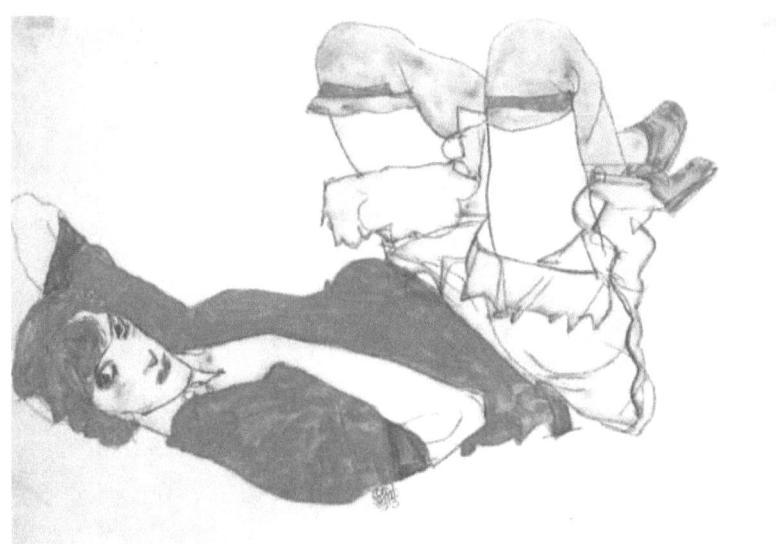

Wally with a Red Blouse
Circa 1913, Watercolor and pencil on paper, Private collection

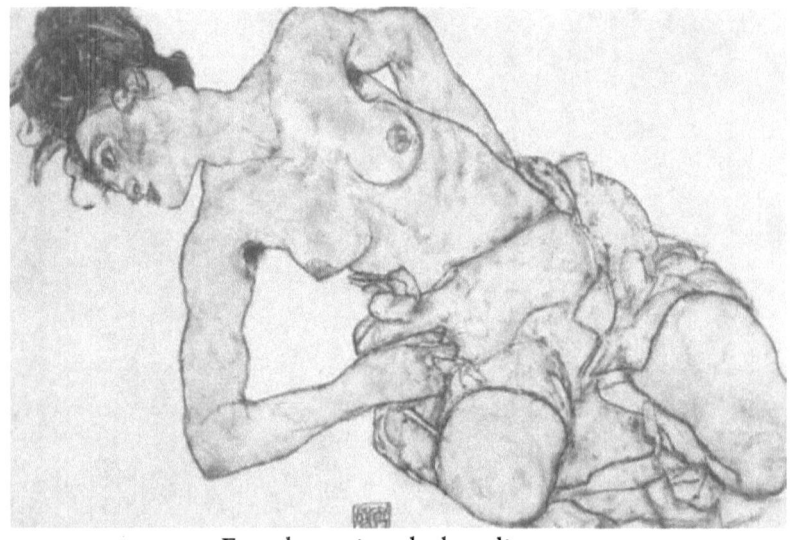

Female semi nude, kneeling
1917, Watercolor and pencil on paper, Private collection

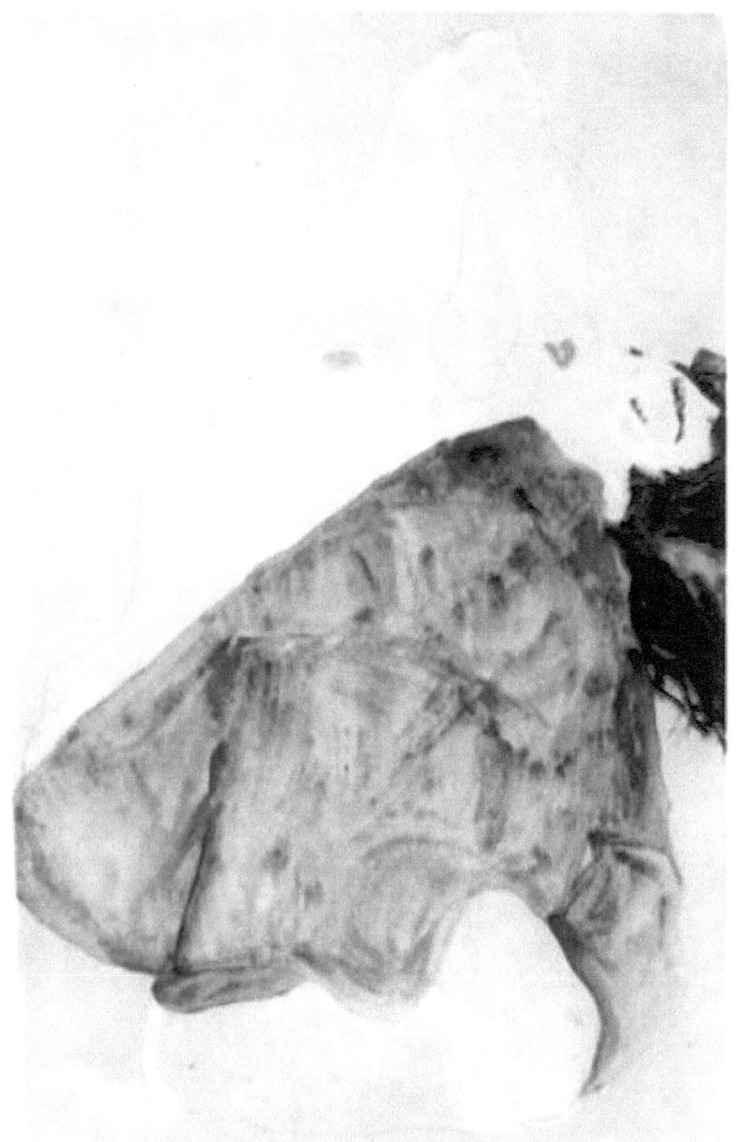

Reclining Nude with purple cloth
1911, Watercolor and pencil on paper, Private collection

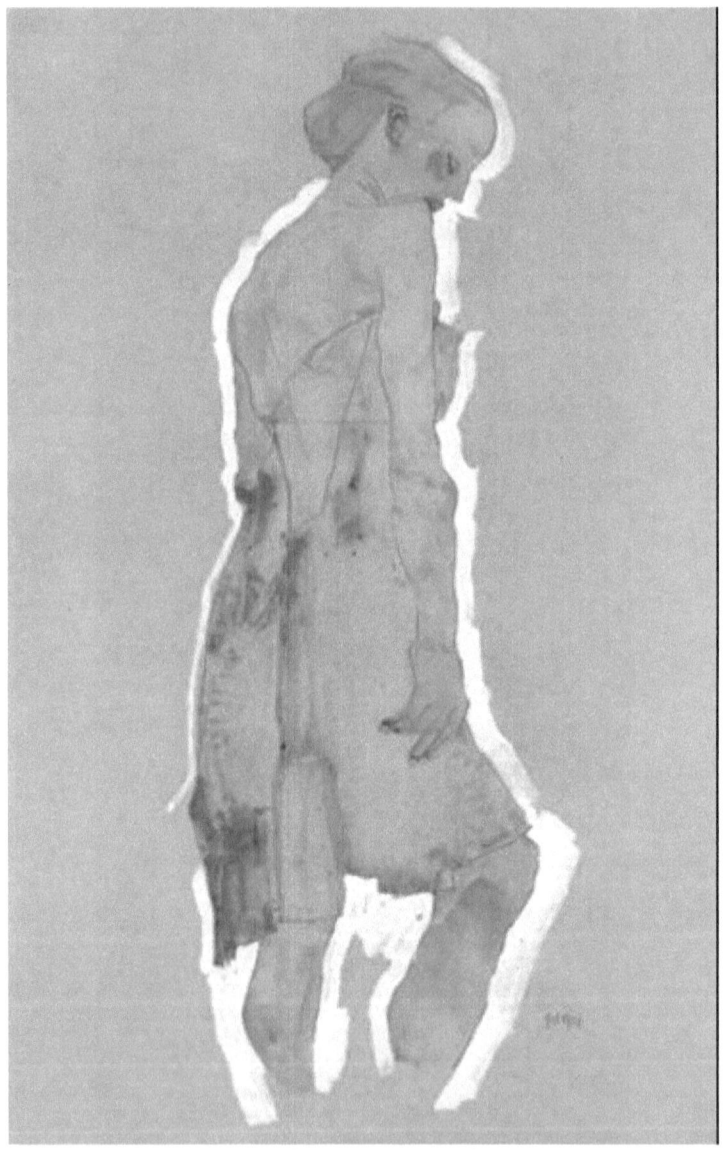

Standing Girl in Profile
1911, Watercolor and pencil on paper, Private collection

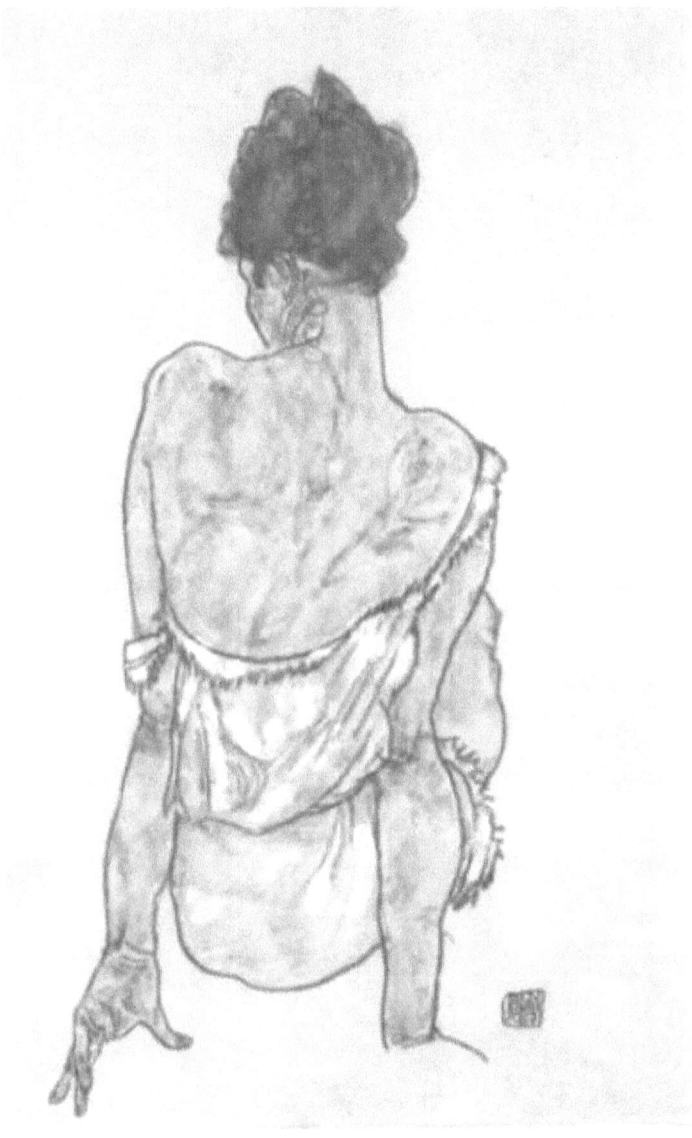

Seating woman
Pencil, watercolor, gouache, 44 x 31 cm, Private collection

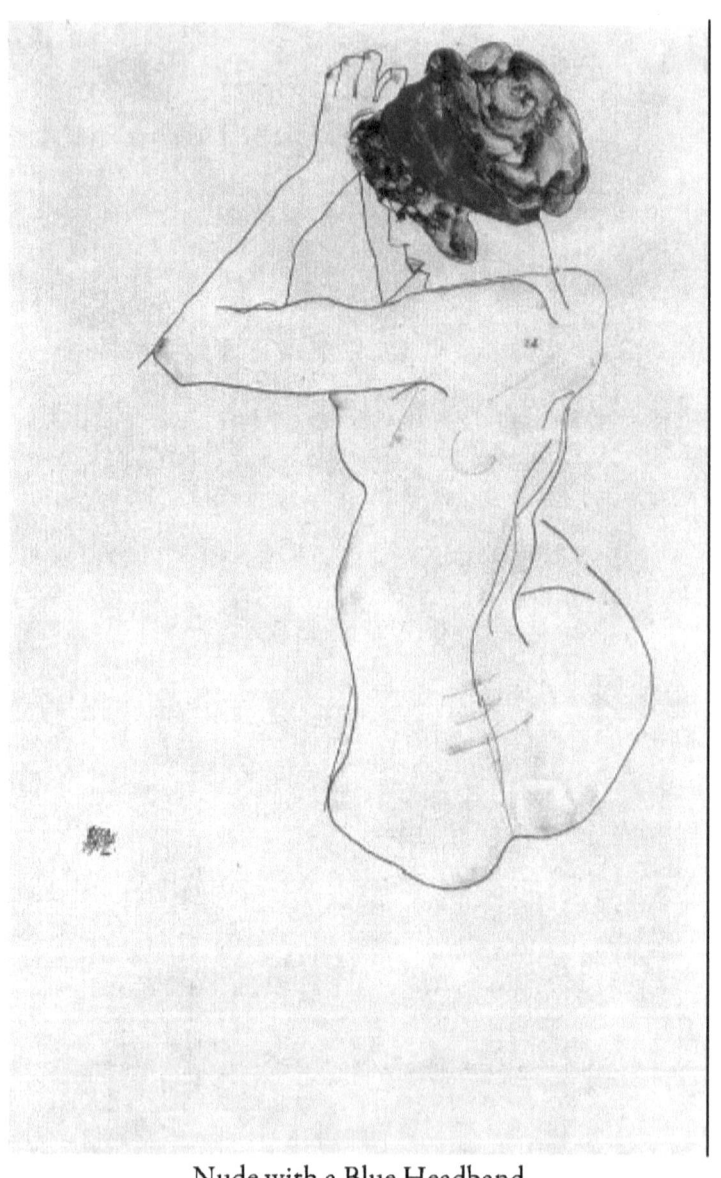

Nude with a Blue Headband
Watercolor and pencil on paper, Private collection

EGON SCHIELE

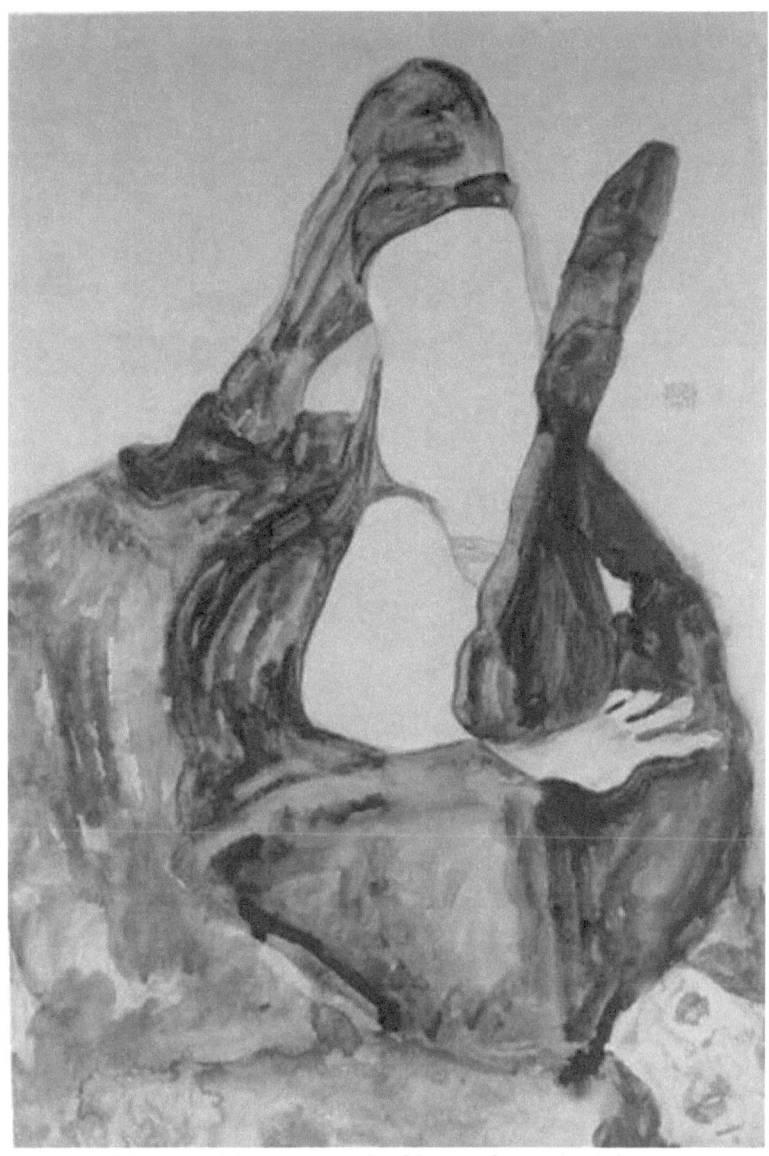

Woman with outstretched leg and purple tights
1911, gouache, watercolour and pencil on paper, Private
Collection

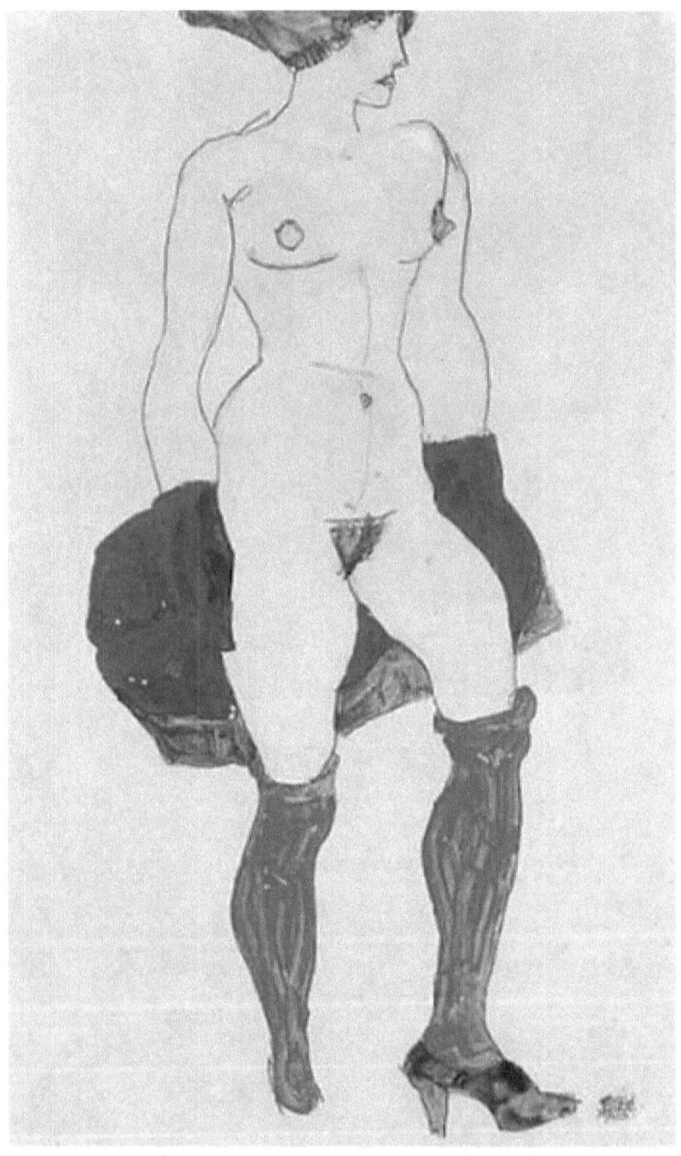

Standing woman with shoes and stockings
1913, gouache, watercolour and pencil on paper, Private
Collection

EGON SCHIELE

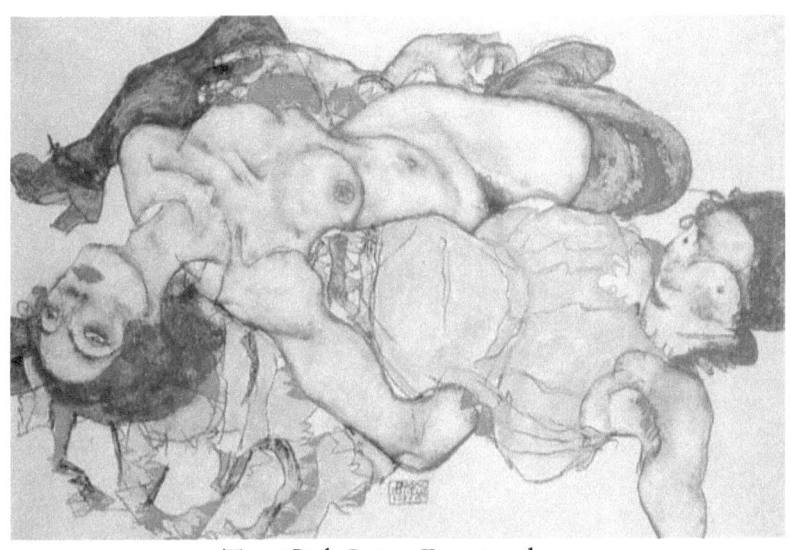

Two Girls Lying Entwined
1915, Gouache and pencil on paper, The Albertina

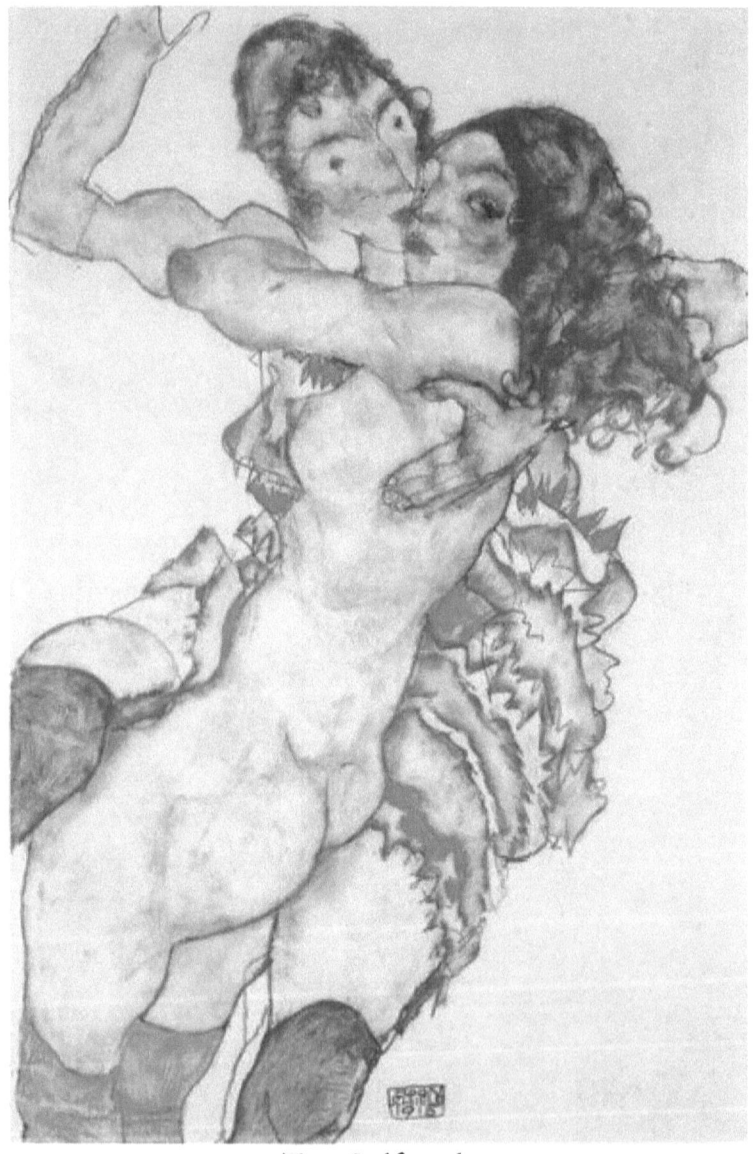

Two Girlfriends
1915, pencil, watercolor, gouache, 48 x 32.7 cm, Museum of
Fine Arts, Budapest

EGON SCHIELE

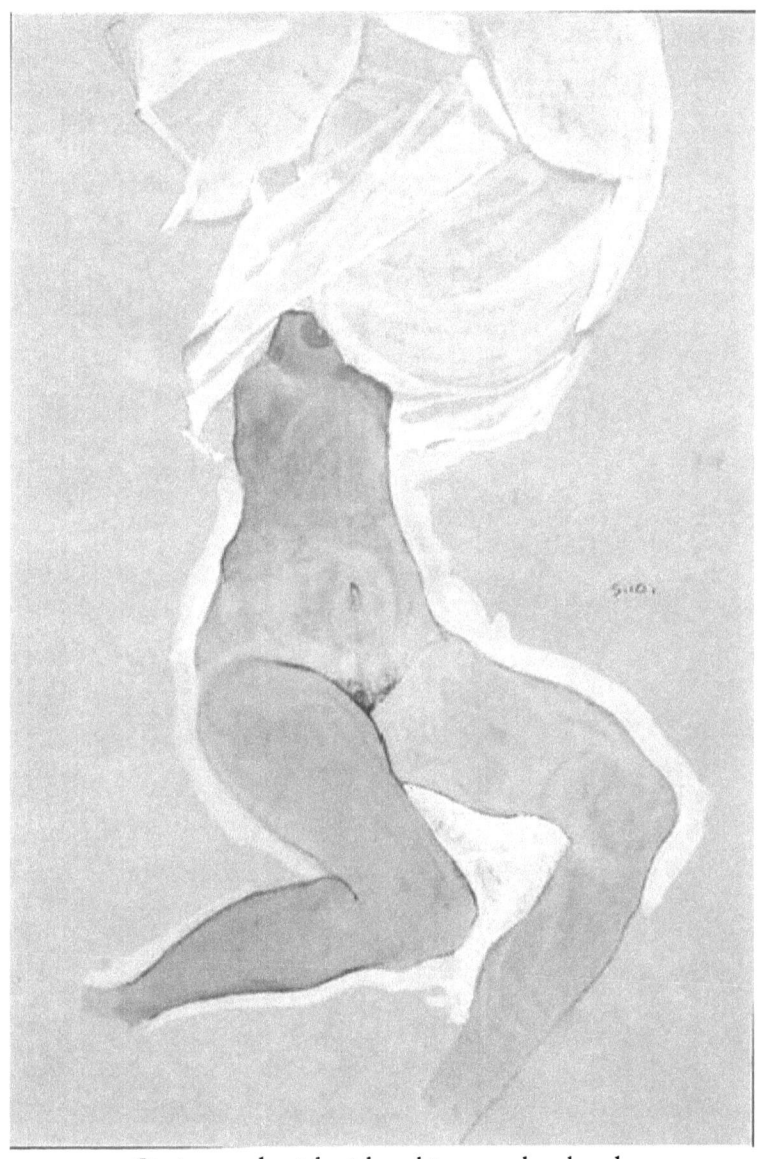

Sitting nude girl with a shirt over her head
1910, pencil, watercolor on wrapping paper, 44.7 x 32.7 cm,
Albertina, Vienna

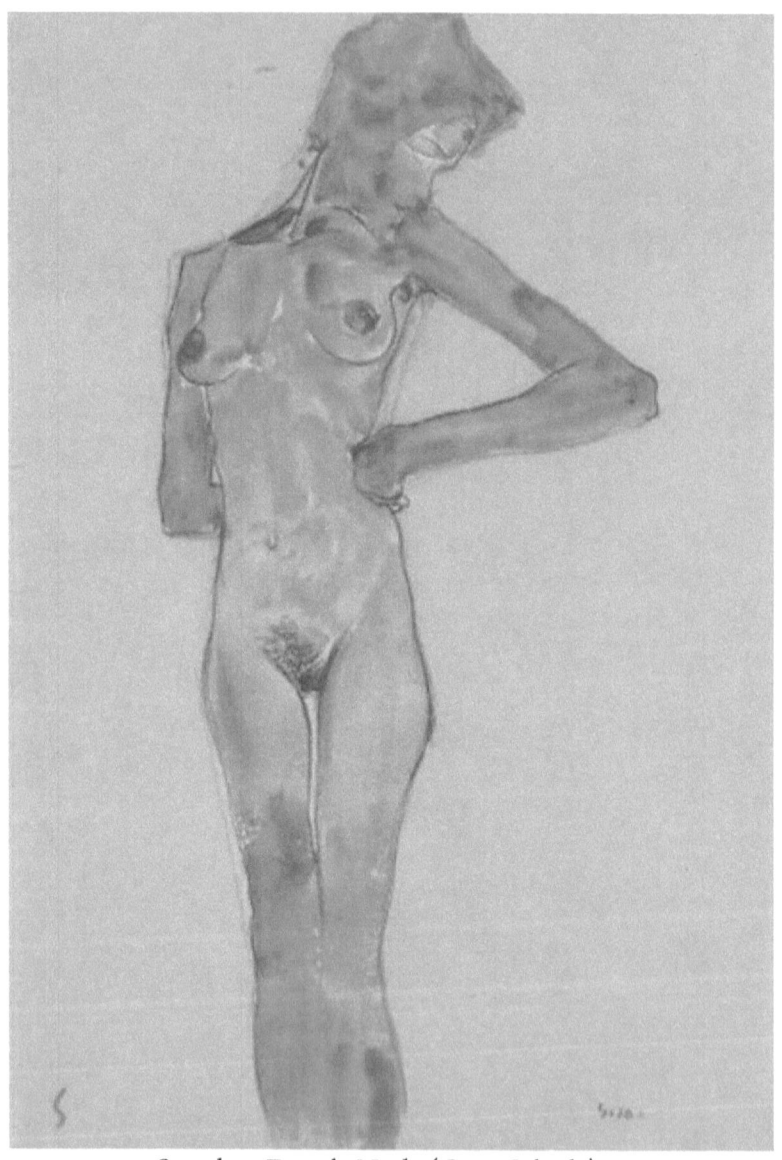

Standing Female Nude (Gerti Schiele)
n.d., watercolor and charcoal on paper, Private collection

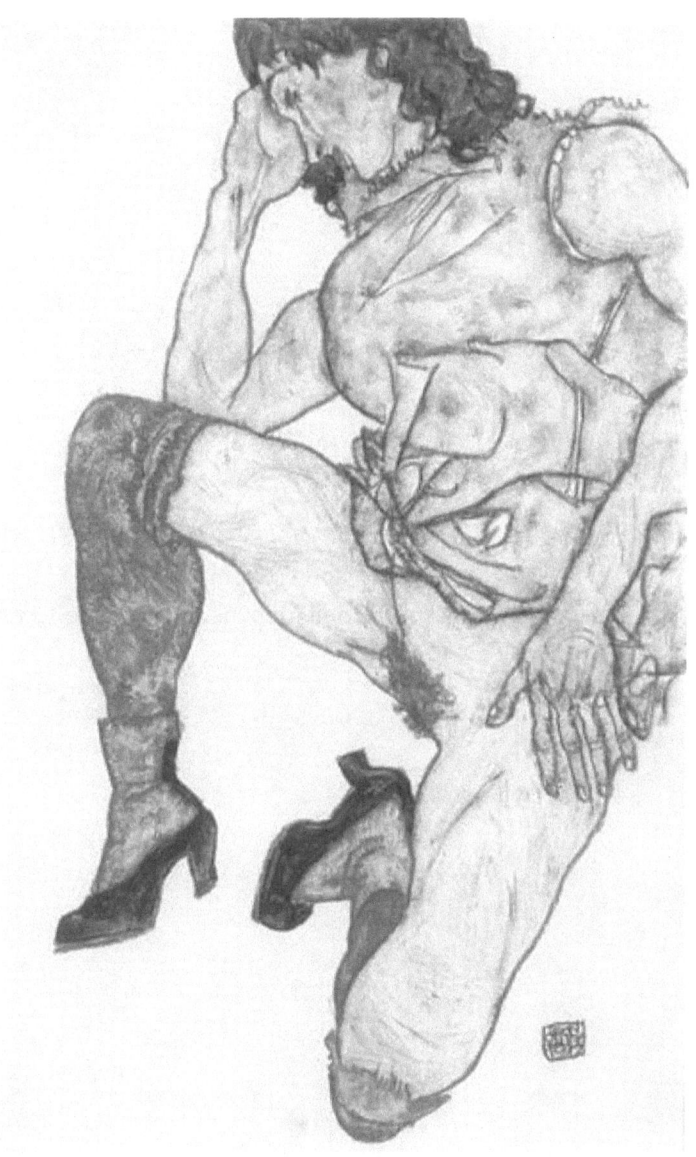

Kneeling girl
1917, Black chalk, gouache, 46 x 28.8 cm, Statliche Graphic
Collection, Munchen

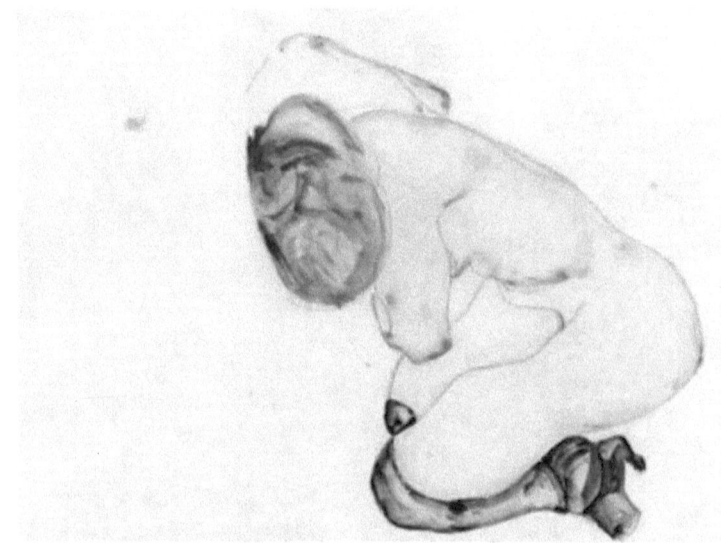

Young girl crouching
1914, watercolor and pencil on paper, Private Collection

EGON SCHIELE

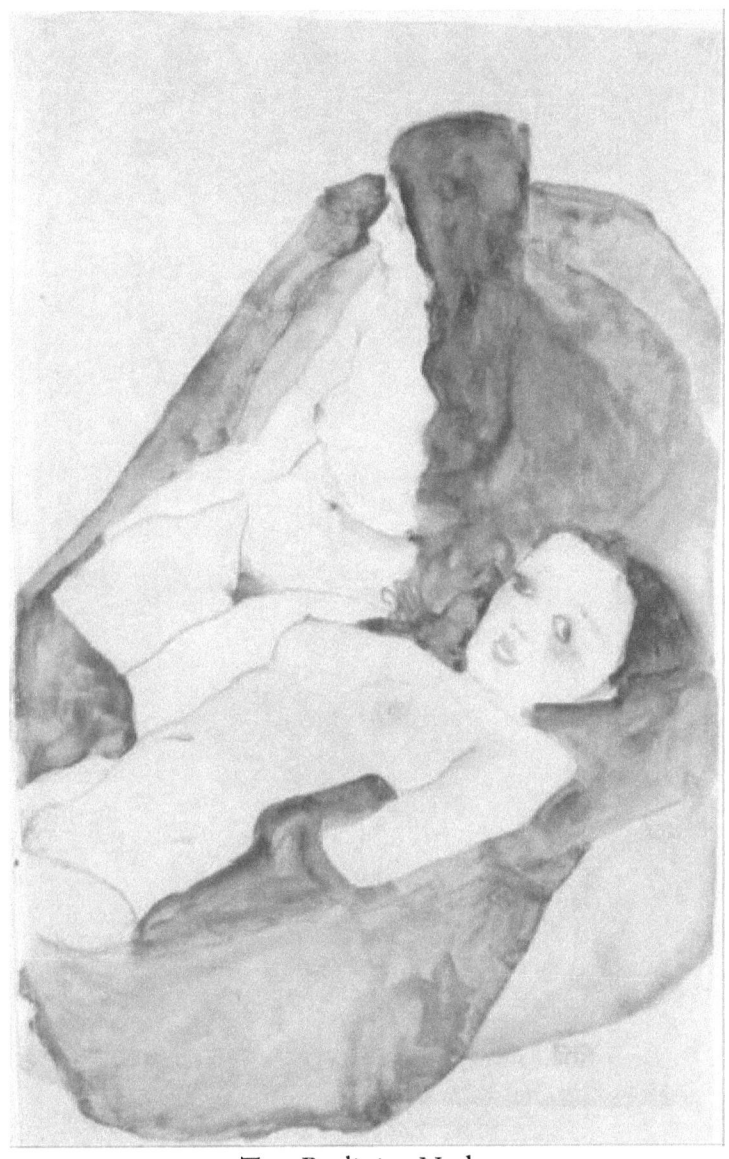

Two Reclining Nudes
1911, Watercolor and graphite on paper, Public collection

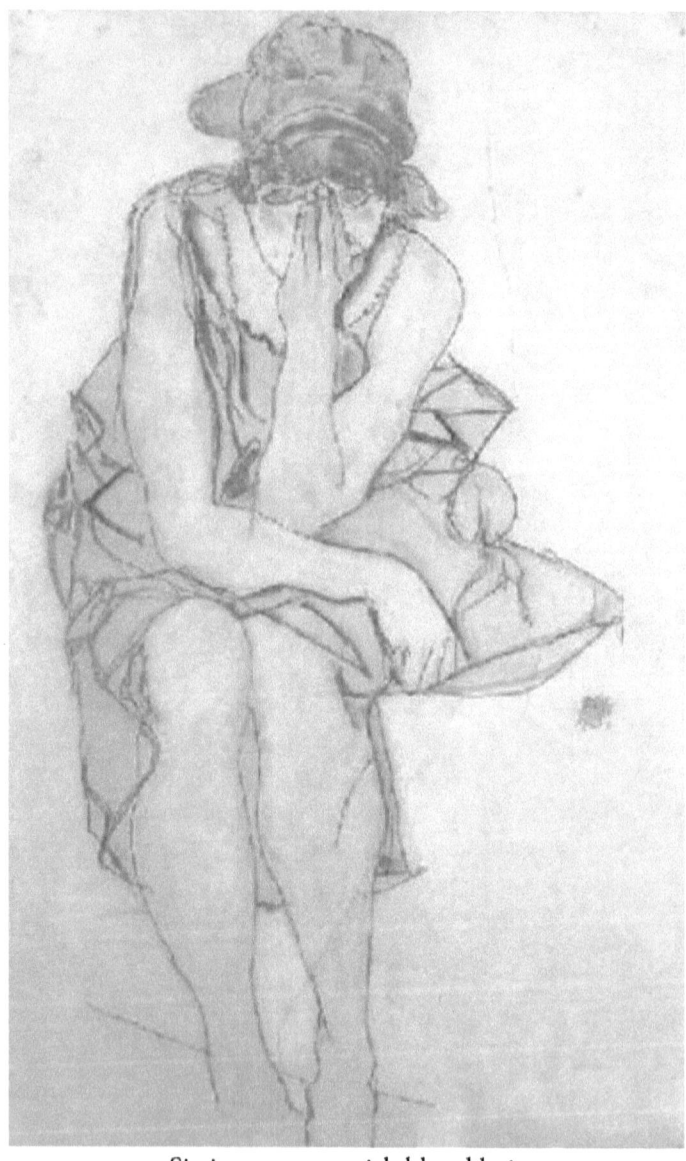

Sitting woman with blond hair
1913, pencil on paper; gouache and watercolour probably
added by another hand, Private collection